The SEED PRINCIPLE

Sowing the Life of Your Dreams

Aubrey Johnson

Gospel Advocate Company
Nashville, Tennessee

Praise for the Seed Principle

"In today's fast-paced, 'anything goes' society, this inspiring book reminds us that character matters and that the Law of the Harvest remains a true force in our lives. – Stephen R. Covey, author of *The 7 Habits of Highly Effective People* and *The Leader in Me*

"Aubrey Johnson's *The Seed Principle* mines profound but practical lessons from Jesus' Parable of the Sower. Beyond the usual applications, Aubrey points us to biblical truths that define true success and show us how to reap the life-harvest we should all desire." – Cecil May Jr., Dean, V.P. Black College of Biblical Studies, Faulkner University

"This warm, wonderful book puts you in touch with your spiritual essence, enabling you to live an empowered life." – Brian Tracy, author of *No Excuses*

"Do you like what you are reaping in your life, relationships, career … ? If not, let Aubrey Johnson show you how and what to sow to achieve the life of your dreams." – Matthew Kelly, *New York Times* bestselling author of *The Dream Manager* and *The Rhythm of Life*

"Aubrey Johnson has provided yet another marvelous offering to improve our lives as we grow in faith. This book utilizes an old, old story from the teaching of Jesus to help us in our efforts to live like Him. This book will bless you and make you a blessing to others." – Jeff Jenkins, Minister, Lewisville Church of Christ

"Aubrey Johnson beautifully uses the parable of the seeds to illustrate a deeply spiritual way of life. Anyone wishing to live more than on the surface of life can benefit from this superb book. It is best read slowly and meditatively. Living its message would mean a life well lived." – Robert E. Wubbolding, Ed.D., Director of Training for The William Glasser Institute and The Center for Reality Therapy

ACKNOWLEDGEMENTS

*Special thanks to my family and friends who read early copies
of the manuscript and blessed me with their feedback:*

Diana Barnhart
Jerry Butler
Dr. Earl Edwards
Dr. Matt Hearn
Neil Hillis
Bill McFarland
David Thompson
Virgil Thurman

DEDICATION

To my grandchildren, Luke, Abby and Levi

*May your hearts be good and noble,
and may your best dreams come true.*

Published by Gospel Advocate Co.
1006 Elm Hill Pike, Nashville, TN 37210
www.gospeladvocate.com

ISBN 10: 0-89225-578-1
ISBN 13: 978-0-89225-578-8

TABLE *of* CONTENTS

The PARABLE
of the Sower

And when a great multitude had gathered, and others had come to Him from every city, He spoke by a parable:

"A sower went out to sow his seed. And as he sowed, some fell by the wayside; and it was trampled down, and the birds of the air devoured it.

"Some fell on rock; and as soon as it sprang up, it withered away because it lacked moisture.

"And some fell among thorns, and the thorns sprang up with it and choked it.

"But others fell on good ground, sprang up, and yielded a crop a hundredfold."

When He had said these things He cried, "He who has ears to hear, let him hear!"

(Luke 8:4-8)

ABOUT
This Book

T *he Seed Principle* is a down-to-earth guide for getting control of your life. More precisely, it explains how you can sow the life of your dreams. Drawing inspiration from the parable of the sower, this book reveals eight proven strategies for harvesting a more abundant life.

The parable of the sower has many layers. On the surface it provides hope for evangelists who wonder if their labors will bear fruit. On a deeper level it is a story about success. It identifies the obstacles you face when trying to influence others, and it sheds light on how you can make desirable changes in your own life.

Using a farming analogy, Jesus explained the process of human growth and attaining goals. You can apply the principles in a shortsighted worldly way or, as they were intended, to develop greatness of soul. In either case, the principles work. How you use them is your choice.

In this parable Jesus explodes two popular myths about success. Success is not a matter of luck or of genius. Rather, success is the result of sowing the right seeds in the right soil. With every choice you make, you sow seeds that produce either weeds (negative results) or fruit (positive results). Consequently, to have the best possible life, make the best possible choices.

Section One: The Secrets

Section One of this book highlights four spiritual laws that explain the way life was designed to work on earth. They are called "laws" because they are unbreakable life principles that regulate all of God's creation. Those who ignore these concepts are continually confused and frustrated by life. Those who learn these laws and put them to good use exercise more control over their lives and enjoy immense blessings as a result.

• **The law of the** *seed* reveals the principle of causation. Causation explains why things happen as they do. The law of cause and effect rules the material world, but it is no less potent in the spiritual world (Galatians 6:7). What you sow is what you reap.

• **The law of the** *sower* shows the possibility of creation. Character and circumstances are largely self-constructed. Humans shape their lives and control their destinies through their day-to-day decisions. Today's choices are the seeds of tomorrow's happiness or regret (Galatians 6:8). Choose wisely.

• **The law of the** *soil* demonstrates the prudence of cultivation. Wise people know that potential must be cultivated to yield its precious fruits. As a result, they tend their souls with the meticulous care of master gardeners. The condition of the heart is the most important factor in producing healthy human growth. Prepare yours well.

• **The law of the** *sickle* underscores the power of continuation (Galatians 6:9). The key to success is perseverance because the harvest comes at the end of the growing season (Ecclesiastes 3:1-2). What is reaped on that day is determined by the seeds you have sown or the opportunities you have blown. Confidence in the law of sowing and reaping inspires consistent effort and endurance. Therefore, the key to success is to sow prudently, plentifully and persistently.

Section Two: The Soils

Section Two of this book digs a little deeper into the soils mentioned in the third law of success. In gardening or landscaping, soil condition can accurately predict whether plants will die, survive or thrive. Jesus identified four kinds of ground and explained how each one affects the growth of seed. He used these soils to represent states of soul. Each one provides a deeper understanding of the way your spiritual condition influences personal growth and the realization of goals. Jesus' message was unmistakable: Preparing the heart is the single greatest opportunity for producing a rewarding life.

• *Hard ground* describes the insensitivity of those who are unaware or unappreciative of truth. Those who are thoughtless or heartless cannot improve their lot in life. Meaningful change begins with acknowledging the need for change. One who does not long for personal transformation cannot succeed in life because growth is fundamental to success.

• *Rocky ground* depicts the condition of the uncommitted. Although enthusiastic, they lack the discipline it takes to follow through. Because progress usually comes through difficult ground, fortitude is essential for moving forward in life. Staying power is the secret to long-term success.

• *Thorny ground* represents those who are unfocused. Their good intentions get lost in a maze of competing interests. Lack of concentration keeps many from enjoying the success of which they are truly capable. New priorities must precede new growth.

• *Good ground* illustrates the integrity of the undivided. It describes men and women whose thoughts and words and deeds are fully aligned. When beliefs, emotions and behaviors harmonize, conditions are right for maximum growth.

Section Three: The Seeds

In Section Three of this book, you will find three practical lessons illustrating how the Seed Principle can be applied in your personal life. If you want to deepen your spirituality, strengthen your relationships, or sharpen your team, you will find just what you are looking for in this section. Use these chapters to move from theory to victory!

• **Sowing seeds for *personal* growth** – Chapter 10 focuses on your growth as an individual because becoming a better person is the key to a brighter tomorrow. This lesson will help you cultivate disciplines that will enlarge your spirit and enlist it in the service of your goals. When inward growth occurs, it enhances every part of your life. Therefore, success begins with spiritual growth.

• **Sowing seeds for *relational* growth** – Chapter 11 will explain how the Seed Principle can be used to enrich relationships with the most important people in your life, to eliminate harmful choices that keep others from drawing close to you. Then one healthy choice at a time, you can nurture a relationship where love and respect increase every day. Friendship and intimacy are not accidents. They are the well-tended gardens of purposeful sowers.

• **Sowing seeds for *organizational* growth** – Chapter 12 applies the Seed Principle to group settings. Because the principles are universal, they will work whether you are building up a church, growing a business, or leading a team of volunteers. Thriving organizations look beyond immediate goals to create a growth environment constructed of positive vision and healthy values.

Checklist for Success

The final chapter will recap the eight essentials for abundant living and provide you with a practical tool for sowing seeds of success in your everyday life. That tool, "The Sower's Almanac," consists of focused questions that enable you to forecast success in reaping the harvest you desire. Using this tool will dramatically increase the probability of positive outcomes by teaching you how to apply the laws revealed in Jesus' parable.

Weed and Seed

At the close of each chapter, you will find resources to enhance your study of this book. Short-answer questions will highlight valuable information to be remembered, and discussion questions will reinforce spiritual principles to be practiced. Next comes the two-part seed and weed assignment. The Seed of the Week is a positive behavior to be cultivated, and the Weed of the Week is a negative behavior to be eliminated. Finally, each chapter closes with a suggestion for personal reflection and prayer. Taken together, these resources will increase your enjoyment of this material, accelerate your growth and hasten your success. You can also visit the website www.theseedprinciple.com for more help. So let's get sowing!

The SECRETS

" **A** nd [Jesus] said to them, 'Do you not understand this parable? How then will you understand [any of] the parables?' " (Mark 4:13). With these words Jesus prepared His disciples to receive the deeper meaning of the sower story. This was no ordinary lesson. Understanding this parable held the key to interpreting every parable. But could it do even more? Might it provide a framework for understanding all of life?

The mysteries of the kingdom of heaven belong to those who understand Jesus' words (Matthew 13:11-12).

- To them more will be given, and they will have abundance.

- To those who do not understand, even what they have will be taken from them.

In Section One of this book, you will encounter four life-changing laws embedded in the parable of the sower. The challenge is to take these laws to heart and consistently apply them in your daily life. Those who love and live these truths enjoy fruitful lives. Those who ignore them suffer repeated disappointment during their days on earth. You can secure your dreams and your destiny by embracing Jesus' message and letting these principles work *for* you instead of *against* you. The choice and the future rest in your hands.

Law One:
Causation (every choice has a matching consequence)

Law Two:
Creation (my choices determine my life experience)

Law Three:
Cultivation (good choices come from good hearts)

Law Four:
Continuation (successful choices require steadfastness)

*"[M]any prophets and righteous men desired to see
what you see, and did not see it, and to hear
what you hear, and did not hear it. Therefore hear
the parable of the sower."*
(Matthew 13:17-18)

CHAPTER 1

God's Word and THE GARDEN *of Life*

> *"When gardeners garden, it is not just plants that grow,*
> *but the gardeners themselves."*
> – Ken Druse, author and garden expert

To live is to choose, and this book is about choosing well. Learning how to choose is important because every decision you make has a real life consequence. Wise choices increase your joy and effectiveness; foolish choices multiply your regret and frustration. The amount of success and sorrow you know on earth relates directly to your choices.

Learning how to make excellent choices is the most important skill you will ever develop. It requires that you take life seriously and live each day attentively. Prosperity and futility hang in the balance with every decision you make. The good news is that plenty of help is available for your training. A fruitful and fulfilling life is possible for anyone willing to be taught. When your heart is ready, the lesson will appear.

The Gardener's Apprentice

The world's first schoolroom was a garden. God placed Adam in the Garden of Eden with instructions to work and keep it. By having him tend the garden, God was teaching Adam more than horticulture: He was providing him with invaluable information about how things grow. The principles Adam learned could be used to cultivate more than corn or chrysanthemums. They provided insight into the way things change for better or worse. He was discovering the power of intention and determined action.

As with Adam, God has placed you in the classroom of life. As you go about your duties, you get the sense that life is about more than laundry and lawn care. Like Adam, you may not understand why you are in your current job or life situation, but God has a plan. There is something He wants you to learn. He yearns to share His wisdom with you, but He waits patiently until you are ready. When that time comes, the Master Gardener invites you to become His newest apprentice.

If God planted the first man in a garden, and Jesus' greatest parable was set in a garden (or field), then a garden must be the perfect environment for learning how life works. From the beginning, gardening has been as much about human growth as plant growth. Successful living, like successful gardening, is about making and managing good choices. Amazing accomplishments, rewarding relationships and commendable character await those who learn the secrets of the sower. The most important lesson to be learned is that the Gardener's words are the seeds of your future success.

Choose Success

However you define it, success is sweet:

- *Strategically* speaking, success means accomplishing a worthwhile goal. Goals may be divided into three categories: having, doing and being. Ultimate success is related to the third category. The person you become is more important than any object you acquire or task you accomplish during your lifetime.

- *Spiritually* speaking, success includes the feeling you get after a dream has been turned into reality – the sense of peace, joy and contentment you experience when significant aims have been met. And more immediately, success is the satisfying emotion that lingers at the close of a well-lived day.

Success can be defined in terms of *process* or *result*: two distinct lenses for looking at a singular event. In terms of process, success involves the ability to get things done – the wise use of your time, energy, attention and resources. In terms of result, it has to do with the feelings created by focused effort. Sometimes calming and sometimes exhilarating, success is the positive emotion that accompanies commendable effort. In the end, though, success will be defined more simply: hearing God's approval and entering heaven's glory (Matthew 25:21, 34).

Life's Ultimate Success Manual

When it comes to the science of achievement, libraries are filled with books that claim to reveal the secrets to tapping human potential. Many contain valuable insights and are well worth the time and money spent to unearth their nuggets of knowledge. However, one book stands head and shoulders above all others in providing the most accurate and helpful information about successful living. That book is the Bible. Why should readers rely on the Bible for securing wisdom about successful living?

• **It came from our Creator.** Because God made humans and the world around them, He possesses incomparable knowledge about the way they function. That beneficial knowledge is made available to men and women in the pages of Scripture.

• **It is inspired.** Unlike most books, the Bible does not intersperse bits of truth with error and opinion. Rather than guesswork or supposition, every page is filled with absolute unmixed truth. The fact that God's Word is completely true is demonstrated in the practical benefits one derives when it is believed and practiced.

• **It has a proven track record.** The Bible has proven its reliability over thousands of years. During that time, countless men and women have attributed their success to faith in God and His Word. From politics to the performing arts, from the boardroom to the classroom, from the laboratory to literary circles, the Bible has left an indelible mark on modern civilization.

Because of its power, Jesus referred to God's Word as "the seed of the kingdom." When it comes to producing abundant life, no force on earth can generate good fruit like God's Word. As an apprentice, your job is to soak up the wisdom of the Master Gardener. Therefore, time spent in God's Word is essential for your success. Your heart is a private garden to be managed for His glory. Trust His teachings, and the day of harvest will justify your devotion to His words.

Old Testament Success Classics

The Bible is not a single book about effective living, but a collection of books about the subject of success. Most bookstores have psychology, self-improvement and other such sections that specialize in helping people live fuller lives. Similarly, the Bible contains many divisions, but each is related in some way to personal growth and practical achievement. Scripture is concerned with your development as well as your destiny.

Law

The first five books of the Old Testament provide foundational life principles for pleasing God and living life at its best. Moses' Law reveals that a great life is defined by great choices. Choices encouraged in the Torah include the following:

- **Genesis** – Successful people choose *faith* (Enoch, Noah, Abraham and Joseph reveal the blessings of walking with God; 5:24).

- **Exodus** – Successful people choose *respect* (the Ten Commandments reveal the wisdom of honoring the rights and needs of others; 20:1-17).

- **Leviticus** – Successful people choose *holiness* (the law code of Israel reveals moral principles that guard souls and societies; 19:2).

- **Numbers** – Successful people choose *gratitude* (the consequences of Israel's discontent reveal the practical value of a thankful heart; 11:1-2).

- **Deuteronomy** – Successful people choose *love* (Moses' final words reveal the necessity of a caring heart for lasting success; 6:1-9).

History

Following Moses' Law are 12 books of history containing real-life stories of people's attempts to live the success principles presented in the Pentateuch. The Lord wants the best for His people and provides them with direction and encouragement to make the most of their lives. God exhorted Joshua, "This Book of the Law shall not depart from your mouth, but you shall meditate in it day and night, that you may observe to do according to all that is written in it. For then you will make your way prosperous, and then you will have good success" (Joshua 1:8).

Prosperity and success are the results of choice rather than chance. Choosing to study God's Word and apply its teachings lays a solid foundation for a satisfying life.

Poetry

The five books of poetry (Job, Psalms, Proverbs, Ecclesiastes and Song of Solomon) are also called "wisdom literature." These books provide understanding for triumphing over life's problems and disappointments. A successful life is not a trouble-free life. Rather, success is found in learning to navigate life's challenges with the compass of faith. Wisdom literature puts today's circumstances in spiritual perspective. It helps people develop more foresight and insight. As a result, they become more reasonable and less reckless. These books provide answers to life's toughest questions and maxims for daily living at its best.

Prophecy

The books of major and minor prophets helped God's people get back on track when they strayed from Moses' teaching. Because keeping the covenant was fundamental to a fulfilling life, the prophets were tireless in calling Israel back to the only foundation for genuine success: commitment to the Lord and His teaching.

New Testament Success Classics

While the Old Testament is a treasure chamber filled with gems of wisdom for intelligent living, the New Testament surpasses it in useful information for attaining a richer experience of life. The beauty and benefits of New Testament Christianity are simply incomparable.

Gospels

Matthew, Mark, Luke and John are a collection of the most fundamental ideals of the Christian faith. In the Sermon on the Mount, Jesus took the eternal principles expressed in Moses' Law to new levels. Christ clarified their meaning and demonstrated their relevance by applying them to contemporary situations. By using stories, Jesus communicated neglected spiritual principles in ways that ordinary people could understand.

However, the New Testament provides more than improved methods of instruction for holy living. The Gospels show righteousness embodied in the selfless life and sacrificial death of Jesus. Christ's charity and integrity resonate with hearts searching for life's meaning.

Acts

The book of Acts is the story of the church's earliest years. The amazing growth of the church demonstrated that Jesus' teachings were true and powerful. However, loyalty to Christ did not guarantee freedom from persecution or problems. During his missionary journeys, Paul faced great adversity, yet he was never without hope (2 Corinthians 4:8-9). Paul's joy in the midst of suffering shows that your inner condition is more crucial to success than your outer circumstances (Philippians 4:4). Success comes from making courageous choices especially during difficult times (James 1:2).

The Epistles

The letters of the New Testament are comparable to the books of prophecy in the Old Testament. Paul and the writers of the general epistles (Hebrews; James; 1 and 2 Peter; 1, 2 and 3 John; and Jude) alternated between exhorting God's people to faithfulness and calling them to repentance. The goal was to urge readers to trust Christ and honor His teachings. These motivational speakers of the ancient world understood that the key to eternal life and effective life was one and the same: heeding God's Word.

Revelation

Revelation closes the Bible's presentation of success principles by stressing the need for steadfastness. Those who remain faithful to the end are assured a victor's crown (Revelation 2:10). But what does it mean to be faithful unto death? It means that as long as there is breath in your body, you must not yield to doubt and discouragement. Like Job, Jeremiah and John the Baptist, you may have delays, setbacks, disappointments and frustrations, but no matter what happens, quitting is not an option. Thomas doubted and Peter denied Christ, but neither surrendered his faith in the end. When fear and despair threaten to sweep over your soul, remember that you can never be counted out when you count on God.

The Crown of Consistency

A crown of life is the incentive to endure in the face of life's obstacles. But "life" here does not refer simply to a length of existence; it refers to a quality of living that is so fantastic it exhausts the imagination. God placed symbols throughout the book of Revelation to hint at the magnificence of this heavenly reward. The blessings of glory include unspeakable beauty and bounty shared in loving community.

Keep in mind that these gifts are not reserved for spiritual superstars with massive intellects, memorable orations and mind-boggling accomplishments. The crown of life is for the sturdy, not the showy; for the durable, not the dramatic; for the steady, not the celebrity. Indeed, faith is the victory that overcomes the world, and nothing says faith like fortitude. Fortitude is the staying power of the soul, the grit of the godly, and the resilience of the righteous. When others are intimidated and demoralized by life, Christians draw on the Lord's power to press ahead bravely (Ephesians 6:10-20). Saints are eternal optimists because they trust in God as the final arbiter of success (Romans 8:31-39).

The Greatest Success Story Ever Told

From beginning to end, the Bible is a book filled with best practices for joyful and fruitful living. The goal of this book is to urge you to spend more time in God's Word and to view its teachings through a new frame of reference: one that demonstrates how you can live the most successful life possible!

With this lens in mind, I will introduce you to the single greatest success story in the pages of Scripture. It comes from the lips of God's Son, who came to share abundant life with those ready to receive it (John 10:10). Those who understand and apply this teaching enjoy richer, fuller lives. The value of this remarkable lesson is reflected in its inclusion in the first three books of the New Testament. Apart from the message of Christ's death, burial and resurrection, it is the most life-changing story ever told.

That story is "The Seed Principle." Some call it "The Parable of the Sower." Others refer to it as "The Parable of the Soils." Whatever you label this extraordinary analogy, it is the ultimate story of success, set against the backdrop of the world's greatest book about success. It brings to light the way in which hope becomes reality and desire becomes destiny. A person equipped with this sacred knowledge can change every sphere of life for the better. It can make a career, rescue a marriage or save a soul. The Seed Principle is a tool. God now places it in your hands. The time has come for you to start sowing the life of your dreams.

Ready, Set, Sow!

In this opening chapter we presented the Bible as a manual for making exceptional choices. Christians are motivated to obey God's commands because those commands are not only true, but also best for producing beneficial results. In every case the best decision is the most loving one. Uncaring choices are the cause of most of the world's grief. The choice to love is the basis for success in all you do.

The parable of the sower is unique in the pages of Scripture because it explains how to make and manage all your choices. The starting point is faith in Christ and His teachings. But even a great decision must be nurtured to succeed. The most promising decision will fail without focus and follow-through. Dream fulfillment requires an enormous investment of time, attention and energy.

By using the four laws of success in Jesus' parable, you can begin putting the power of the Seed Principle to work in your life today. And by understanding the four soils of the spirit, you can turn your heart into fertile ground for fulfilling your deepest desires. If you are ready to start sowing a more satisfying life, then turn the page and welcome the seed of God's Word into your heart. You will be amazed by the harvest to come.

"While the earth remains, Seedtime and harvest, Cold and heat,
Winter and summer, And day and night Shall not cease."
(Genesis 8:22)

Questions

1. What is the most important skill you will ever develop?

2. Why is learning to choose well so important?

3. What do foolish choices multiply?

4. What do wise choices increase?

5. What is the best book ever written about successful living?

6. Give three reasons why the Bible can be trusted as a guide to successful living.

7. Why did Jesus refer to God's Word as "the seed of the kingdom"?

8. What private garden do you manage for God's glory?

9. What new frame of reference was suggested for reading your Bible?

10. Which parable is the greatest success story ever written?

Discussion Questions

1. Explain the opening phrase of this chapter: "To live is to choose."

2. How is the amount of success one knows on earth related to his or her choices?

3. What can a person learn about life from spending time in a garden?

Assignment

Seed of the Week: Love

Seeds can be thoughts, words or deeds. Before you leave class, make up your mind when and where you will sow at least one small seed of love this week. But remember: He who sows bountifully will reap bountifully!

Weed of the Week: Selfishness

Think of a time when you frequently demand your own way. Now decide that when this situation occurs, you will be more flexible and generous. Be on the lookout for random acts of selfishness you can eliminate.

Reflection and Prayer:

What do you reap when you sow more love and less selfishness on a daily basis? Ask for God's help to stay intensely focused on this goal for seven days. Each week begin your class session in small groups, spending five or 10 minutes discussing how you did with your seed and weed assignments.

CHAPTER 2

The Law of
THE SEED
The Principle of Causation

"Though I do not believe that a plant will spring up where no seed has been, I have great faith in a seed. Convince me that you have a seed there, and I am prepared to expect wonders."
– Henry David Thoreau

From the beginning of time, a law has been in operation that has determined the course of events upon the earth. That law, "The Seed Principle," is the law of life. It guides the physical growth of plants and animals, and it directs the psychological and spiritual development of human beings. This principle affects the body, mind and soul. Moreover, it explains the past, maximizes the present, and predicts the future.

It is no accident that the Seed Principle made its first literary appearance in the opening chapter of Genesis. From the beginning of time, it has been recognized as the fundamental law of God's creation. Moses wrote:

> Then God said, "Let the earth bring forth grass, the herb that yields seed, and the fruit tree that yields fruit according to its kind, whose seed is in itself, on the earth"; and it was so. And the earth brought forth grass, the herb that yields seed according to its kind, and the tree that yields fruit, whose seed is in itself according to its kind. And God saw that it was good. So the evening and the morning were the third day (Genesis 1:11-13).

When God introduced plants into the world on the third day of creation, He also unveiled the organizing principle of the planet He made. In an almost offhanded statement, Moses remarked that plants would be governed by a divinely established law of reproduction: *Each would bring forth after its kind.* This seemingly insignificant statement revealed the primary law that guides the entire universe. It gave an order and predictability to life that wise men and women have leveraged for success ever since.

Humans began to reason, "If apple seeds produce apple trees and acorns produce oaks, then perhaps I can use this lesson from nature to develop my own nature." Can this principle really be transferred to the mental and moral realm? Can it help you tend the garden of your life? Will it show you how to cultivate your character and harvest happiness? The answer is a resounding yes! If you decide what you want in life, plant the appropriate seeds, and nurture their growth, you can shape your own future.

The Nature of Seeds

The most important thing to remember about seeds is that they contain life. A plant produces a fertilized seed containing an embryo that will germinate under the right conditions. When the seed reaches the right temperature and receives the right amount of moisture, it begins to sprout. But what a seed produces is predetermined by its parent. Every plant must bring forth after its own kind.

The Seed Principle is equally at work in the animal kingdom. The seed of a monkey does not produce a moose, and the seed of an owl does not produce an orangutan. Life and likeness are the nature of seeds. They generate and replicate. Every seed contains both energy and identity.

Yet even more amazing is the application of this principle to the realm of thought. In addition to biological seeds, there are ideological seeds. Although unseen, these spiritual seeds are real and intensely potent. By influencing the mind, they shape the material world. Clearly, information exerts a force that excites emotion and action.

Good ideas are packed full of power to unleash human potential. Like water rushing through a dam's turbines, thoughts run fluidly through the mind producing electrifying insights. And yet water must turn the blades of the turbine's engines to generate energy. Likewise, thoughts that do not lead to action are wasted like water over a dam. Good intentions, wishful thinking and daydreaming travel down the spillway of the mind. They come and go and are soon forgotten. However, ideas that prompt action are a dynamic force for change. They are the current that sparks initiative and the power that drives achievement.

The Seed of the Kingdom

When we think about power, several images immediately come to mind: electric generators, jet engines, nuclear power plants. But who would ever think of a seed? When Jesus thought about power, His mind turned to the mustard seed. When planted, this tiniest of seeds virtually explodes into a sturdy tree where birds rest and animals seek shade. Moreover, Jesus said this amazing feat of nature is comparable to the growth of His kingdom.

Jesus declared, "The seed is the word of God" (Luke 8:11). When God's Word is planted in receptive hearts, the results alter life and destiny. The change is so dramatic that bona fide believers are said to be born again (1 Peter 1:22-25). But spiritual rebirth is not merely a figure of speech. It is the dynamic consequence of holy ideas blossoming into reality. A new person emerges as one places himself under the Lord's influence. When God reigns, lives change, and that change is so thorough and complete that a Christian is said to be a new creation (2 Corinthians 5:17). The planted gospel generates a higher level of thinking that initiates life and sustains growth.

If life and likeness are the essence of a seed, then Christ's teaching qualifies in both respects. Jesus told His disciples, "The words that I speak to you are spirit, and they are life" (John 6:63). Physical existence qualifies as "life" only for those who are thinking on the lowest level. In fact, those who are controlled by their bodies' desires are dead in sin (Ephesians 2:1; 1 Timothy 5:6). The Word of God is life-bearing because it releases moral and spiritual energy under the right circumstances. This higher quality of life is one of blessedness that reaches all the way into eternity. It is both abundant and everlasting.

Faith is the catalyst that unleashes the life force within the seed. Paul wrote, "For this reason we also thank God without ceasing, because when you received the word of God which you heard from us, you welcomed it not as the word of men, but as it is in truth, the word of God, which also effectively works in you who believe" (1 Thessalonians 2:13). To work effectively, the Word must be embraced. That is why the gospel is the power of God unto salvation for all who believe (Romans 1:16). No belief, no power and no salvation. The seed is no less potent, but its power is reserved for another time, another place, another person where its life force will be discharged with success.

Good Seeds and Bad Seeds

George Washington declared, "Bad seed is robbery of the worst kind: Your pocket-book not only suffers by it, but your preparations are lost and a season passes away unemployed." Substandard seed wastes a farmer's money, labor and time, but shoddy spiritual seed is even more costly. The price of investing in inferior ideas is a waste of spiritual potential.

Educator Russell H. Conwell wrote, "I ask not for a larger garden, but for finer seeds." Conwell understood that it takes superior seed to produce exceptional fruit in the garden of the mind, and he was convinced that the purest and finest intellectual seeds come from Scripture. Many religious and philosophical ideas compete with God's Word for people's confidence, but they cannot produce an equal effect.

Thoughts are psychospiritual seeds that produce deeds. Therefore, by controlling their thinking, people exercise control over their lives and futures. Any creative force with the power to duplicate itself is a kind of seed. That is why Paul urged his followers to choose their thoughts carefully (Philippians 4:8). Thoughts that are true, honest, just, pure, lovely, virtuous and praiseworthy produce lives of the same noble quality. Right thinking is the key to right living. Consider these statements:

- Healthy thoughts produce wellness by leading me to care for my body.

- Holy thoughts produce goodness by encouraging me to consult my values.

- Happy thoughts produce gladness by prompting me to count my blessings.

Conversely, hateful, hopeless or hedonistic thoughts will lead me to behave in ways that damage my health, self-esteem and relationships. Ralph Waldo Emerson remarked that "thoughts are the seed of action," but deeds themselves are also seeds on a more complex level. Deeds are the fruits of thought but the seeds of habits. Habits are behaviors repeated so often they become second nature and no longer require conscious thought. Attitudes are merely habitual ways of thinking. Character is habit of mind and life so entrenched that it cannot be changed without considerable effort. When patterns of thought and behavior become deeply rooted, few possess the will to surmount them. Therefore, the sooner a person engages in purposeful thinking and intentional living, the better.

Primary Beliefs

All sorts of ideas are spread through the media, Internet, pulpit, classroom and by word of mouth. They are like seeds carried to distant places by wildlife and the wind. Some are true, and others are blatantly false. Some are helpful, and others are appallingly destructive. Knowing this, Jude urged his readers to contend earnestly for the faith once delivered to the saints (Jude 3). Jude understood that beliefs make a difference in the quality of a person's life and his eternal destiny.

The challenge each person faces is selecting a basic set of beliefs that will produce the best life possible. These foundational beliefs serve as a filter to screen out harmful or useless information and speed decision-making. They are the bedrock of success or failure in life. In fact, the most important thing a person will do on earth is select his primary beliefs, because every future thought, word and deed will spring from this fundamental choice.

Although you make many decisions during your lifetime, some are definitely more important than others (Matthew 23:23). No doubt the choice of what to have for supper is not as earth-shattering as selecting the community where you will raise your family. And the choice of paint colors for the house is not as critical as selecting the spouse who will parent your children.

Paul understood that the most crucial decisions you make are spiritual. Spiritual decisions form your worldview and determine the course of your future. Consequently, Paul singled out faith, hope and love as the most enduring qualities of a successful life. Each is a choice, and choosing to trust God, think optimistically, and care deeply for others are foundational components of personal fulfillment.

Choice Categories

The beliefs that allow you to navigate life fall into four main categories: duty, integrity, identity and utility. Choices in the first two categories form the basis for choices in the latter ones. Therefore, by deciding weightier matters first, subsequent decisions become easier (Matthew 23:23). Reversing the order complicates your life and limits your success. The order is vital. To live successfully, choose sequentially.

Category 1: Duty

The most basic set of choices you will make concern your worldview. Your view of the world and your place in it spring from a handful of questions that allow you to make sense out of life. To find your purpose, ask:

- Where did I come from?
- What am I doing here?
- Where am I going?

These inquiries into your origin, mission and destiny lead you to faith in God or to a philosophy of life that overshadows your entire existence. It is the most foundational choice anyone makes and the one requiring the most careful deliberation. Happiness and heaven await those who choose wisely.

Category 2: Integrity

The second cluster of choices concerns your values. To form healthy values, ask, "What is truly important in life?" According to Jesus, two things are of supreme value in this world: your soul (Matthew 16:26) and your relationships (22:37-39). Every other virtue grows out of these priorities (Romans 13:9). Next to God, people are the most precious thing in your life. The challenge is to keep first things first (1 John 2:15-17).

The New Testament's lists of ethics clearly reflect the priority of loving God and those created in His image. Review the passages below, and note the way they promote love and safeguard associations.

- The Beatitudes (Matthew 5:1-12)
- The love chapter (1 Corinthians 13:4-7)
- The fruit of the Spirit (Galatians 5:22-23)
- The armor of God (Ephesians 6:13-18)
- The Christian virtues (2 Peter 1:5-7)

Category 3: Identity

The third group of choices allow you to express your individuality. Over time these transformational choices shape and reveal your unique personality. They play the greatest role in creating the circumstances in which you live out your life.

Decisions in this group are not easily undone; thus their consequences are far reaching. Most of your joy or misery can be traced to this handful of decisions. And choices at this level always raise bigger questions that must be answered to select the best option.

- Will I marry? Whom will I marry? (*What is the reason for marriage?*)
- Will I have children? How many? (*Why have children?*)
- Who will be my friends? (*What is the meaning of friendship?*)
- Which career will I choose? (*What is the purpose of work?*)
- What are my goals and priorities? (*What do I care about most?*)
- How will I use my free time? (*What is the point of recreation?*)

Category 4: Utility

The fourth class of choices is related to day-to-day functioning. These are the transactional choices that allow a person to operate as a human being. Christians must guard against these concerns becoming all-important (Matthew 6:25). Examples of this type of question are:

- What will I eat?
- What will I wear?
- What will I drive?

Although not as crucial as choices in previous categories, they are still quite revealing. They are glimpses into your personality and soul. Your worldview and values are evident in the way you spend your money and your days. When these choices are compatible with Christian beliefs, they produce peace and progress. When incompatible, they create conflict and confusion. Abundant living, therefore, is the natural consequence of making choices consistent with faith in Christ.

Mind Games

Children often believe they can get by with bad behavior and escape any consequences if they are cunning enough. They invest their energy in not getting caught rather than in doing what is right. It is the job of parents to teach them the impossibility of evading responsibility for their choices no matter how shrewd they may be. No intricate system of lies and excuses can free people from experiencing the results of their decisions. The sooner this lesson is learned, the happier and more satisfying life becomes.

As an adult you are accountable for the quality of your life. Regardless of your childhood experiences, the moment has come to finally grow up. It is time to stop playing games and to start thinking with clarity and purpose. It is time to be more intentional about the choices you make and the seeds you sow. The time has come to put strategic action ahead of wishful thinking.

When you expect to reap what you never sowed, disappointment waits around the corner. Attitudes of entitlement are the essence of immaturity and a waste of precious life. Childishness of this kind is unbecoming of adults. It is unattractive to your spouse, infuriating to your boss, and unacceptable to your God. If you are ready to get on with the business of life, the next chapter will tell you how to retake control by assuming responsibility for your choices and their consequences.

Questions

1. What is the Seed Principle? Where is it first found in the Bible?

2. What is the most important thing to remember about seeds?

3. What do seeds contain besides life?

4. Name two kinds of seeds.

5. What analogy was used to represent thoughts that do *not* produce action?

6. What analogy was used to represent thoughts that *do* produce action?

7. What image did Jesus choose to convey the idea of power?

8. What is the catalyst that releases the power contained in God's Word?

9. What forms the bedrock of a person's success or failure in life?

10. Name the four categories of choices.

Discussion Questions

1. How does the Seed Principle explain the past?

2. How does the Seed Principle predict the future?

3. How does the Seed Principle maximize the present?

Assignment

Seed of the Week: Joy

Decide when and where you will sow at least one small seed of joy this week. Notice how it makes you feel and how others respond. You will discover that seeds of joy can multiply rapidly.

Weed of the Week: Unhappiness

Unhappiness has more to do with your thoughts than your circumstances. What thought has created the most unhappiness in your life recently? It is time to pull the weed! Stop fixating on facts of life you cannot change, and sow thoughts that are positive and constructive. Remember, it is your mind and your choice.

Reflection and Prayer:

What do you reap when you sow more joy and less unhappiness on a daily basis? Ask God to help you think more joyful thoughts for the next seven days.

CHAPTER 3

The Law of
THE SOWER
The Possibility of Choice

"Only God can make a tree,
but I'm in charge of seeds and weeds!"
–Author unknown

It is one thing to understand the principle of causation and quite another to grasp the power of personal choice. It is the difference between the victim and the victor, the casualty and the conqueror, the whiner and the winner. The realization that you can initiate positive change in your life and in the world around you is both exhilarating and empowering. God has placed the future in your hands, and your decisions are the seeds of your destiny.

Admittedly, you have little control over some things. You cannot choose your parents or the time and place into which you are born. Nor can you directly determine the choices of others that impact your safety and happiness. In a sin-compromised world, calamities of nature and collapses of social responsibility exist that exceed your control.

Yet consider the breadth of choices God has placed within your reach. You can choose your attitude and response to each of life's events. You select your friends and the spouse with whom you will journey through life. The way you treat other people and, therefore, the quality of your relationships is up to you. You pick which books and periodicals to read (Paul, Plato or *Playboy*). The school you attend, the major you pursue, and the career you choose are your prerogative. You decide whether to invest your time or waste it. Will you save money or spend recklessly? Will you prepare for eternity or live carelessly? You choose whether to finish the course or throw in the towel.

Life is nothing more than a series of choices. Circumstances are the evidence or fruit of those choices. The orderliness of your life, the holiness of your character, and the peacefulness of your soul reflect the values upon which those choices were based.

The Sower as Seer

There are many possible futures, but only one will come to pass. To live effectively you must figure out what you want and pursue it. Those who do not know what they want are lost. The clearer your vision, the more likely it will come to pass. Productive people have a compelling mental picture of where they are headed and the difference they want to make in the world. Underachievers lack direction and motivation because their purpose and goals are hazy.

This principle is plainly illustrated by the life of the sower. Good gardening begins with good planning, and good planning begins with keeping the end in mind. Every other factor depends on the result one hopes to achieve. Is the goal a pumpkin patch, an apple orchard, or a field of corn? Countless issues cannot be settled until the end is in view (seed, soil and spacing). Working backward is the only sensible way to pursue a farmer's goal. The realm of personal or professional growth is no different. Beginning with the end in mind is the only decent way to live.

That is why every person must come to terms with the purpose of life. Is there an eternity to be prepared for, or does existence end abruptly at death? Are money and pleasure the greatest ends of life, or is serving others more important and satisfying? Do I have a unique talent that suggests the best use of my time, or is climbing the corporate ladder the summit of success?

Through inquiry, observation and reflection, a purpose begins to emerge that gives meaning and direction to life. Just as the colorful, neat rows of a well-tended garden first existed as an idea in the planter's mind, so you must believe in a life of beauty and benefit before it can become reality. Worthwhile achievements and godly attributes are not accidents. They are the outgrowth of aspiration and the fruit of faith.

The Sower as Selector

Good planning must be followed by good planting. Once you know what you want, you are ready to begin sowing the life of your dreams. The need will determine the seed. The key is to move continually in the direction of your objective by sowing seeds (thoughts, words and actions) that will bear the desired fruit. The more you make wise choices, the more quickly you are propelled toward your goal. The more you make foolish choices, the less likely it is that you will ever reach your objective (James 1:2-8; Genesis 1:11). When coming to a fork in the road, do not ask, "Which path is the longest or most difficult?" Instead, ask, "Which path will carry me to my desired destination?"

Making choices at cross purposes with your goals is as counterproductive as planting briars in a garden. The harvest day will be disappointing, and the barbs are bound to inflict wounds (1 Timothy 6:10). Those who fail to live strategically are ignoring the law of the sower. They do not live with purpose and intention. They see life as a mystery rather than a responsibility. Those who live wisely make principled decisions based on their vision and values. They think:

- Long-term rather than short-term
- Systemically versus symptomatically
- Relationally instead of selfishly

Choose Who Will Sow Into Your Life

In the Sermon on the Mount, Jesus applied the law of the sower to the realm of human relationships.

> Beware of false prophets, who come to you in sheep's clothing, but inwardly they are ravenous wolves. You will know them by their fruits. Do men gather grapes from thornbushes or figs from thistles? Even so, every good tree bears good fruit, but a bad tree bears bad fruit. A good tree cannot bear bad fruit, nor can a bad tree bear good fruit. Every tree that does not bear good fruit is cut down and thrown into the fire. Therefore by their fruits you will know them (Matthew 7:15-20).

The nature of religious teachers is evident in what they produce in the lives of those around them. Jesus said by their fruits you will know "them." Therefore, the Seed Principle is an excellent tool for weighing the words and gauging the character of people who want to influence you. Some seek intimacy. Others crave authority. But how can you tell the difference between the trustworthy and treacherous? The answer lies in their fruit.

Learning to judge fruit is important because all people sow seeds into the lives of those closest to them (1 Corinthians 15:33). All profess the best of *intentions*, but *outcomes* separate a good influence from a bad one. Captivating charisma, convincing words and charming good looks are not the best criteria for making sound judgments about people. Look at the fruit, not the façade. This is the closest you can come to looking within the soul of another. Fruit always mirrors its source.

Contrary to popular opinion, it is not wrong to judge others. Judging motives and destinies is God's business, but judging fruit (effects or results) is everyone's business. Only the most immature and unstable neglect this responsibility. But be careful how you judge! What is wrong is prejudging others based on superficial information or personal bias.

Whether choosing a bride, baby sitter, best friend or business partner, discretion is advisable. Lack of due diligence may result in injury and inconsolable loss. Judging fruit is not only fair but Jesus says it is also necessary. It is a divinely approved means for detecting the phony with a ravenous appetite for self-advancement at the expense of others.

However, the best use of the Seed Principle is for self-examination. Paul implored, "Do not be deceived, God is not mocked; for whatever a man sows, that he will also reap" (Galatians 6:7). The link between what is reaped and sown is unbreakable. Frustration and failure are the direct result of self-deception in this matter. If I believe I can sow one thing and reap another, I am deluded and bound to be disappointed.

Choose What You Will Sow Into the Lives of Others

Whenever you speak to someone, you are planting seeds; therefore, weigh your words carefully. Words are verbal seeds that contribute to the success or failure of the one you address. Your remarks are implanted in the heart of your hearer. They take root there, grow and produce fruit. And like all seeds, your words produce after their kind.

When my wife, Lisa, and I would put our three boys to bed at night, we would spend time playing a special game called "I love you more than … ." The idea was to see who could outdo the other in the most extravagant expressions of love. One would say, "I love you more than chocolate." The other might reply, "I love you more than doughnuts." The game was fun, but the goal was vital: planting seeds of certainty that each son was deeply loved. We would close by giving a kiss and a hug and offering one final reminder: "You know I will never stop loving you."

What subliminal messages would you like playing in the background of your child's mind? What secret tapes would you like running beneath his conscious thought? What hidden voice and encouraging words would you have him hear wherever he may travel throughout life? The quality of these clandestine conversations goes a long way in forming the character and self-esteem of your child. Plant your seeds carefully, for what he hears in his soul is bound to grow.

Whether you are speaking to a child, spouse, friend or co-worker, all people long to be treated with dignity and respect. By relating to them in terms of their potential rather than their past, you help them expect more of themselves. And by viewing them as valuable and capable, you empower them to move beyond their previous limitations. Believing in others and caring deeply for them is the secret to healthy relationships. It is the key to success in marriage, parenting, teaching, coaching, managing, preaching or shepherding. Encouragers are people who consistently sow seeds of confidence in those closest to them.

Sow a Great Attitude

In addition to sowing seeds in others' lives, every individual sows into his own mind. In fact, your attitude is merely the fruit of past dialogues with yourself. But regardless of your past outlook on life, you can adopt a healthier, more positive frame of mind whenever you choose. Paul urged his readers, "Rejoice always, pray without ceasing, in everything give thanks; for this is the will of God in Christ Jesus for you" (1 Thessalonians 5:16-18). These words describe the Christian mindset and God's means for cultivating it:

- Rejoice always (*the target*)
- Pray without ceasing (*the tool*)
- In everything, give thanks (*the tactic*)

God wants His children to experience boundless joy throughout their lifetimes. Unfortunately, many Christians are willing to settle for a lot less. Exhibiting joy is one of the best ways a believer can let his light shine before a discouraged world. A person who is deeply, genuinely happy stands out like a bright star in the night sky. But far too often, joy is the missing link in evangelism.

To live a life of abiding joy, two things are necessary. First, prayer must permeate each day. Joy is not possible without pausing to collect your thoughts and focus them in a more spiritual direction. The more Bible-based and God-centered your thinking, the more joy it produces.

Second, attention should be directed primarily to your blessings. Our natural tendency is to look for what is wrong in a situation. God wants His people to reverse that trend by looking first for what is good and beneficial. Measurable benefits flow from counting your blessings. Thankful people are friendlier, healthier and more energetic. They drink less, depend on fewer medications, and sleep better at night. Research confirms that gratitude produces a better quality of life.

Gloominess, on the other hand, has more to do with bad choices than bad genes. So why not choose to join the ranks of the grateful? In the morning, start your day with a *gratitude shower* that will lift you up as you lather up. In the afternoon, take a *gratitude stroll* that will increase your happiness as you elevate your heart rate. In the evening, make an entry in your *gratitude journal* to turn off bad thoughts as you drift off to sleep.

If you are prone to find fault with people and grumble about your circumstances, God has a plan to break you of these habits: *Give thanks in everything*. In other words, make gratitude your default attitude. Be the first person to put things in perspective when "bad" news arrives. Take the lead in pointing out blessings and opportunities when challenges arise. If you are a pessimist or chronic complainer, please understand this is not God's will for you. He wants you to stop your negativity and tells you precisely how to do it. Learn to look on the bright side without ignoring the dark side. Be honest, but frame things in the most hopeful way possible. Rather than reverting to your old habits, you could:

- Identify something positive in the current situation and share it.
- Offer constructive solutions to address the need at hand.
- Say something supportive about the ideas of others.
- Volunteer to lead or assist in resolving the problem.
- Put your full weight behind whatever the team decides.

Being a thankful person is pleasant and profitable, but it is not easy or natural. Cultivating an appreciative life is a spiritual discipline that must be developed. There are many ways to do it, but all of them have one thing in common: They force you to focus your thoughts in a more thankful direction. By redirecting thought, gratitude can transform things you take for granted into precious gifts (James 1:17). By sowing seeds of appreciation, you will reap unlimited joy, and this is God's will for you.

Sow to Achieve Goals

While sowing a superb attitude is crucial, sowing is equally vital for molding character, improving relationships and changing circumstances. People who know exactly what they want and stubbornly sow to that end vastly increase the probability of getting what they desire from life. On the contrary, vague aims and inconsistent effort undermine desired outcomes.

High levels of productivity demand a combination of clarity and energy, but neither can sustain progress by itself. Hazy goals and hard work can rarely produce success. And half-hearted efforts in pursuit of well-defined goals yield only occasional results. But who wants random success? The parable of the sower reveals the secret behind predictable patterns of success. Clear objectives and obstinate effort are the stuff of fulfilled dreams.

Suppose a person wants to become an exceptional teacher. Once a firm decision has been made, a path begins to emerge. What degree or certification do I need to do the job? Which schools are recognized for their expertise in this field of education? Are there professional groups I can join to shorten my learning curve? What additional skill sets can provide me with a strategic advantage? Is there a code of ethics I must adhere to? How should I dress to project the right image? Whose acquaintance should I make to increase my chances of securing a desirable position? Who might I approach to be my mentor? Regardless of the vocation, the formula for improving your situation is basically the same. Growth and achievement involve a calculated succession of small steps that move one closer to a well-defined objective.

Without clarity is a lack of *direction*, and without energy is a lack of *action*. Fruitful living is not a fluke, but the result of steadfastly sowing the right seeds. It is not fate or good fortune. Success is the end result of three things: faith, follow-through and focus.

The Sower as Surveyor

More will be said in the next chapter about the importance of good soil for the growth of seed, but a word should be said here about the importance of soil selection. The sower decides where to distribute his seed in keeping with the harvest he hopes to produce. Some plants do well in shade while others need full sun. Some are impervious to frost, and others are resistant to heat. Good seed in the wrong climate or soil conditions will never flourish. A wise gardener is careful to sow in the right place.

Similarly, a prudent person spends more time working on his strengths rather than his weaknesses. Areas of giftedness are the most fertile soil for producing a useful life. Everyone has unpleasant tasks on his schedule, but it is possible to minimize that list through staffing, delegation and role refinement. And the sooner the better for everyone involved. Greatness is becoming more of who you really are, so remember to sow to your strengths.

Similar care should be taken to develop fruitful relationships. Sadly, many people squander their time trying to salvage ties with people who are abusive. A boss, friend or love interest who is cruel, demeaning or opportunistic should be told his behavior will not be tolerated. Hazardous working and dating relationships should be terminated at once. Do not minimize or rationalize the dehumanizing behavior of others. Limit your exposure to their antics and look for healthier horizons. Seek out new job opportunities and friendships where you will be respected and valued as a person. You will be happier when you do.

The point is not to run away from your problems, but to recognize the difference between what is solvable and intractable. Distinguish between people who are immature (irritating) and those who are unsafe (destructive). Keep your patience with the former, and keep your distance from the latter. When dealing with the cruel and callous, Jesus advised, "Do not cast your pearls before swine" (Matthew 7:6; Proverbs 11:22).

The Sower as Supplier

In addition to choosing the *kind* of seed one will sow, God allows a person to determine the *amount* of seed he will sow. Some sow frugally while others sow lavishly. When it comes to dreams, sowing meagerly is shortsighted because what is harvested will be in direct proportion to what was sown. When a person hopes to reap what he never bothered to plant, he is out of touch with reality.

Successful people are prolific sowers. They understand how life works and take advantage of this knowledge by sowing aggressively. Paul wrote, "But this I say: He who sows sparingly will also reap sparingly, and he who sows bountifully will also reap bountifully" (2 Corinthians 9:6). The law of reciprocity says that if I want to receive something, I must first give something. With few exceptions, sowing must precede reaping. This makes perfect sense in a world governed by cause and effect.

Jesus promised, "Give, and it will be given to you: good measure, pressed down, shaken together, and running over will be put into your bosom. For with the same measure that you use, it will be measured back to you" (Luke 6:38). In other words, success has more to do with being a go-giver than a go-getter. Strategically speaking, it makes sense to give what you hope to receive. If you want the respect of others, then give respect. If you desire the trust of your team, then grant them your trust. If you want the love of your family, then love them first. When you are rude, distrustful and selfish, is it any surprise that you receive in kind?

Having said this, however, one should understand that it is a mistake to believe happiness can come from a what's-in-it-for-me mindset. Successful people love giving for its own sake. It is their nature and delight to contribute something valuable to the lives of others. Experience has taught them "it is more blessed to give than to receive" (Acts 20:35). Therefore, they help others without keeping a tally and expecting payback (Luke 6:35). Following Jesus' example, they distribute seeds of love without demanding anything in return.

The Sower as Supervisor

Once a sower plants his seed, the work is far from done. Careful supervision is required for reaping the best possible harvest. Assessing and addressing the needs of growing plants is the ongoing responsibility of a successful farmer. Similarly, careful oversight is essential to making the most of your life and decisions.

In most cases, the difference between a good choice and a bad one is what you do after the initial choice has been made. Monitoring and managing decisions is nearly as important as making them in the first place. Incessantly second-guessing yourself is unhelpful. Perfect choices are pure fantasy, and pursuing these figments of the imagination will only produce inaction or dissatisfaction.

The disgruntled Israelites wasted an astonishing amount of time looking back nostalgically on their former lives in Egypt. "If only" is a game for losers. Instead of complaining about the present and glorifying an imperfect past, focus on ways to improve the current situation.

In sports, coaches modify their game plans. In aviation, pilots correct their flight plans. In warfare, generals adjust their battle plans. In most cases, small swift changes are the pathway to success. A tiny change in a timely manner is the winner's way. It may not be showy or spectacular, but if results are what you are looking for, steadiness is what works.

There is definitely a time in life for making a bold move, reinventing yourself, or starting over from scratch, but these moments are the exception rather than the rule. Most of the time, success is a slow, gradual process comparable to gardening. It is the culmination of countless little things you do in the determined pursuit of your dreams, the combination of vigilance and diligence over the course of a lifetime.

Conclusion

The day you realize you are responsible for the content of your character and the circumstances of your life is the day you finally grow up. Expecting others to take care of you is perfectly natural for children but unbecoming of adults. It is the hallmark of immaturity. The truth is that no one will care for your body, marriage, career, retirement or soul like you will. When you stop demanding that others secure your happiness, you will finally be free to take charge of your life.

The key to success is recognizing what you are choosing. Linking choices and consequences gives you leverage for creating the life of your dreams. Yet many choose to live in a world of fantasy rather than reality. They eat and spend and drink and work and talk and drive like there are no consequences. They do not ask, "What will this choice do to my health, relationships, goals or future?"

Your experience reveals what you have chosen in the past. If you do not like what you see, then a new set of choices is in order. And even when you feel you have no choice, real options are on the table if you look a little closer. When your first choice is unavailable, a more difficult one may be required. If you cannot change your circumstances, then a change of attitude may be needed. When all the choices before you seem unpleasant, remember that "those who sow in tears shall reap in joy" (Psalm 126:5). Trust God, keep the end in view, and keep sowing.

Questions

1. What is the most revolutionary insight of which a person is capable?

2. What lies beyond a person's direct control in a sin-compromised world?

3. What word was used to describe a person who does not know what he wants?

4. How do good gardeners begin their work?

5. Worthwhile achievements and godly character come from what two things?

6. What propels a person toward the realization of his goals?

7. What does a foolish person ask when approaching a fork in the road?

8. What does a wise person ask when coming to a fork in the road?

9. In most cases, what is the difference between a good choice and a bad choice?

10. What two things underlie predictable patterns of success?

Discussion Questions

1. How can it be said that "life is nothing more than a series of choices"?

2. Why is it crucial to figure out what you want in life?

3. How is greatness the result of becoming more of who you are?

Assignment

Seed of the Week: Peace

When and where will you sow at least one small seed of peace this week? This may require putting relationships ahead of getting your way. When tensions arise, break the cycle with a goodwill gesture or repair attempt.

Weed of the Week: Strife

Arguments seldom produce what a person desires. Even if you get what you want, you must deal with lingering resentment and a damaged relationship. Express your desires frankly, but remove yelling, threats and punishment from your negotiator's tool kit.

Reflection and Prayer:

What do you reap when you sow more peace and less contention on a daily basis? Ask God to help you be a peacemaker whenever conflict arises over the next seven days.

CHAPTER 4

The Law of
THE SOIL

The Prudence of Cultivation

*"To be a successful farmer, one must first
know the nature of the soil."*
– Xenophon, 400 B.C.

On the third day of creation, God said, "Let the waters under the heavens be gathered together into one place, and let the dry land appear" (Genesis 1:9). Separating the earth and sea provided a setting for seeds to sprout and mature. God said, "Let the earth bring forth ..." (v. 11). Good soil makes growth possible.

Soil does this by providing support and sustenance for developing plants. To stand erect, a force must be exerted to keep stems in place. Otherwise they will lean and eventually collapse. Soil also retains moisture to refresh plants and contains nutrients to sustain them. Plants use their roots to eat and drink, and soil holds the food and water essential for development.

The term "soil" generally refers to that portion of ground on the surface of Earth that sustains the growth of plants. It is a mixture of rock, mineral and organic matter, water and air. Soil ends approximately at the point where native plants reach their maximum rooting depth and biological activity ceases. In other words, life is what makes Earth's soil. How fitting, therefore, that Scripture uses the idea of soil to illustrate the ground of spiritual life and growth.

Spiritual Parallels

Jesus saw amazing similarities between the life-supporting work of the ground and the life-sustaining work of the human heart. Using a parable He began to draw out the comparisons between four soil types and soul types. Before looking at the specific applications, some general observations are in order.

First, the seed and soil analogy is especially striking when one recalls that human beings were created from the dust of the earth (Genesis 2:7; 3:19). People are animated earth or soil in motion. Second, fruitfulness is the goal of life. Just as the earth was made to receive seed, renovate it, and return something new and improved to the world, so human hearts were made to give as well as to take.

Once the life-giving seed is embraced, it must interact with the varied components of spiritual soil. The fertile heart, like fertile ground, is multifaceted, combining cognition, emotion and resolution. Each element must act in concert for the seed to accomplish its purpose. No single part will do. Mind without heart produces legalism while heart without mind produces subjectivism. Favorable fruit requires interaction with all the constituent parts of the soul: heart, mind and will.

The need for spiritual balance can be illustrated by political science. In America three branches of government were designed to take care of the people's business. The legislative, judicial and executive branches were intended to complement each other and guard against potential abuses by any single part. When these divisions work in unison, the result is progress. When they do not, the result is gridlock. Sin involves an imbalance of power of the spiritual kind. Growth comes to a standstill when the body overrules the brain or feelings undermine faith. Indeed, the wages of sin is deadlock.

Purpose and Passion

People who know what they want and why they want it will usually find a way to succeed. Unfortunately, many people lack the clarity, commitment and concentration necessary to seize life's opportunities. They never take time to figure out what they want, so they settle for the trinkets of a temporal world. They start things but seldom finish because they lack motivation. They do so much that they fail to do what matters. Successful people are just the opposite. They focus on important things and not just the pressing or pleasing. They make commitments carefully because they know that less can be more. They enjoy the compounded interest of their labors by persevering long enough to reap what they sow.

Jesus began His parable with these robust words: "A sower went out to sow." The sower was an agent of change equipped with intention and initiative. He knew exactly what he wanted and took strategic action to produce the desired result. He was deliberate and dynamic. But as the parable continues, it reveals that something more is needed. Without good soil, the sower's efforts go for naught. When it comes to spiritual growth, beginning well is critical, but long-term success requires a good heart and not just a good start.

Growth Environments

Terrestrial

All growth requires a proper environment. For example, most planets in Earth's solar system lack a suitable atmosphere to support life. No plants or animals have been found on their surface because of a lack of water and air. The temperature is either too cold or hot for living things to survive. As a result, they are referred to as dead planets. In contrast, Earth flourishes with countless life forms due to its extraordinary ecological balance. But if this delicate system were disturbed, the consequences would be disastrous.

Educational

In education, young students need a good academic environment to excel scholastically. This setting begins with a competent and caring teacher. Next comes a supportive principal to assist the classroom instructor. But the most important element of successful education is parental involvement. When any of these ingredients is missing, the learning process is compromised in some way. An apathetic parent, weak administrator or inept teacher can cause a gifted student to underperform and settle for mediocrity.

Commercial

In business, the A Team can become an F Team if any of its members is unethical or underachieving. A distracted CEO, dishonorable CFO or divisive COO can keep a company from reaching its projected earnings. When A Team members effectively communicate and cooperate, they create a dynamic culture that boosts morale and productivity.

Ecclesiastical

In churches, a healthy atmosphere is no less important for growth. In Ephesians 4:11-13, Paul described the positive environment needed to unleash the potential of God's people. To reach Christian maturity, a team effort is essential. The body of Christ is "joined and knit together by what every joint supplies, according to the effective working by which every part does its share, causes growth of the body for the edifying of itself in love" (Ephesians 4:15).

Intrapersonal

Yet even more important than a safe and stimulating church environment is the condition of one's own spirit. In matters of this kind, the internal always takes precedence over the external. When it comes to growth, ground zero is the human heart (Luke 8:15).

Soil Conditions

Strictly speaking, Jesus' parable concerned itself not with different soil compositions but soil *conditions*. Whether a particular soil is good or bad depends on the plant you are trying to produce. Soil types are determined by the amount of sand, silt or clay they possess. Sand particles are large, silt particles are medium, and clay particles are small. The size and shape of the particle determines how it drains and how many nutrients it can hold. Wisteria grows well in sandy soil and pyracantha in clay.

Like soil, personalities are unique, but each plays a valuable role in the growth of God's kingdom. This means that the main problem facing humans is not congenital (type A vs. type B) but conditional. When it comes to assessing your spiritual condition, three questions cut straight to the chase:

1. How broken is your spirit?
  Am I open to improvement?
2. How deep is your love?
  Am I committed to improvement?
3. How free is your heart?
  Am I attentive to improvement?

For beneficial change to take place, you must overcome the obstacles of denial, doubt and distraction. If you are unwilling to change, insufficiently motivated to change, or lack clear priorities for change, success is improbable.

Like a game of 20 Questions, Jesus chose images from three broad categories (animal, mineral and vegetable) to make His point. Birds, rocks and weeds are the figures He used to illustrate how spiritual growth may be thwarted. And problems can come from multiple directions. Sometimes they come from above (hungry birds), and at other times they come from below (hidden rocks). But most often they come from beside or within (hurtful thorns). With so many points of attack, vigilance is the watchword.

How we view the parable depends on where we see ourselves in the story. It can be viewed from multiple angles depending on the identity of sower and soil. Each person must ask, "Which am I?" And at times the answer will be, "Both." Frequently, it is your own heart into which you sow.

Growth Inhibitors

The point of each illustration is that something is preventing the seed from reaching its potential by depriving it of the room and resources needed for growth. In the first instance, no place is found for the seed to take root. In the second case, limited room is available as the seed is let in partially. In the third example, the seed is allowed all the way in but is eventually outpaced by plants of lesser value.

Although the obstacles to growth are relevant, the central issue is the receptivity and productivity of the human spirit. Whether I am closedminded, small-minded or absent-minded makes little difference if no fruit ultimately grows. Whether the seed is stolen, scorched or strangled is beside the point. *How* spiritual barrenness occurs is of secondary importance; *that* it occurs is of primary importance. An unfruitful life reflects an unrefined heart. Therefore, cultivating the heart is the God-given responsibility of every individual. It is job No. 1 in life.

The Lord will not accept half-hearted love, faith or commitment. He wants your entire heart. He demands wholeheartedness because nothing less will produce the abundant life He desires for you. He is disappointed when you settle for half of your potential because doing so also means settling for half of the joy and usefulness that could be yours. Your perfection is His glory. This means He wants the very best for you – not selfishly, but for your fulfillment and the benefit of the world that desperately needs you to be your best self.

Growth Incubators

The God of heaven is devoted to growing things. In the beginning He planted Adam and Eve in the Garden of Eden, and although their mistakes were prodigious, they grew in love for God and one another. The Lord planted Israel in the land of Canaan, and although they sometimes lost their way, they were a shining light in a dark world.

No earthly environment is perfect, but God continues to provide people with surroundings to stimulate their growth. His desire is for marriage to provide an intimate environment that will draw out the best qualities of a man and woman. He intends for a loving home to bring forth the gifts He placed in a newborn baby. And in the church, He plants each family, couple and single person where loving shepherds will guard their souls, guide their minds and comfort their hearts throughout a lifetime of growth.

Ultimately, though, the heart is the ground of all meaningful growth. God's Word and His church can help to raise your consciousness, strengthen your resolve and purify your spirit. When things go awry, the gospel can provide a way back to the person you were meant to be. It can soften hard hearts, deepen shallow hearts and unite divided hearts. Yet, for all the resources God puts at your disposal, the deciding factor will always be your own desire to grow. That is why abundant living is:

- more about improvement than achievement;
- more about growth than goals; and
- more about becoming than doing.

Prepare for Greatness

Dreaming expands the heart, mind and soul. Therefore, it is good to dream. Doing so is neither selfish nor frivolous. In fact, God encourages you to dream big (Ephesians 3:20). But be careful what you dream. Some dreams stretch the spirit, while others shrink it.

Some dream about a beautiful home for raising a family and extending hospitality, but be careful if you obsess over square footage and amenities. There is nothing wrong with wanting a safe, dependable car with a value that outlasts its payment book, but be wary if you are preoccupied with speed and status. It is fine to dream of watching a sunset on a tropical island with someone you love (and to contemplate what you will do with your deeper love upon returning home), but watch out if your island adventure is about letting down your hair without answering to anyone.

James counseled Christians to beware of consumer-oriented, lust-based dreams (James 4:1-3). But he assured those who long for the fulfillment of their legitimate needs that God will bless their desire for growth and contribution to His kingdom. Take a moment to compile a list of the things you desire that will bring lasting joy to your life and to those closest to you. Refine your dream list from time to time to be sure it grows along with you, and do not forget to celebrate your progress.

Dream Lists

People dream about having, doing and becoming many things. The motives behind those dreams are as important as the dreams themselves. Ask yourself, "Why do I want this?" God is not offended when a person desires new carpet, an ocean cruise or a college education. However, He wants His children to know the difference between primary and secondary goals.

The best goals are spiritual rather than material. They are about strengthening the soul rather than pleasing the body, and about service rather than self-interest. Great dreams are about character, connection and contribution. Some dreams are very personal, but others should be dear to every person's heart. My dreams for you include the following:

1. Closeness to God

2. Someone to love and nurture

3. A friend who challenges you to be your best

4. Confidence to live and speak authentically

5. Work you cannot wait to do each day

6. Respect for your body and its needs

7. Appreciation for the value and limits of your time

8. Control of your tongue and temper

9. More time making memories with those you love

10. Courage to be your true and best self

Great dreams are about growth rather than worldly pleasure or gain. They are about relationships rather than riches or revelry. When the heart is properly prepared, it supports you in the pursuit of your dreams. But a person who is hard-hearted, half-hearted or heavy-hearted with worldly cares will find it difficult to sustain a satisfying life.

Solomon wrote, "As snow in summer and rain in harvest, so honor is not fitting for a fool" (Proverbs 26:1). In other words, some things simply do not go together. The chances of encountering an honorable fool are about the same as having a blizzard in July. People who ignore God's laws will find success and the respect that follows to be elusive. Although a fool may have moments of seeming success, he will lack the necessary grounding for enduring success. Solomon understood that reputation and admiration are not accidental. Honor is the fruit of a well-cultivated heart.

Questions

1. Where does soil end?

2. What is the purpose of soil?

3. Name three parts of the heart that must work together to be fruitful.

4. What three images did Jesus use to illustrate threats to the seed?

5. What is the common problem behind the three unproductive soils?

6. What central issue is Jesus addressing in the parable of the sower?

7. Name three ways the seed is kept from achieving its purpose.

8. In what environments do couples, babies and Christians grow?

9. What is the ground (spiritual soil) of all meaningful human growth?

10. Name three kinds of minds that will never reach their potential.

Discussion Questions

1. Which of these questions is most relevant for you: How broken is your spirit? How deep is your love? How free is your heart?

2. Why do people tend to set material rather than spiritual goals?

3. Which dreams from the dream list most appeal to you at this time?

Assignment

Seed of the Week: Longsuffering

When and where will you sow a small seed of tolerance this week? Remember that being right is not a justification for flying off the handle and treating people disrespectfully. Consider how patient and forbearing Christ has been with you.

Weed of the Week: Impatience

In what situation have you been short-tempered recently? Don't get caught off guard next time. Imagine yourself remaining calm and composed. Rehearse how you will respond with restraint. A deep breath or a short break can do wonders.

Reflection and Prayer:

What do you reap when you sow more peace and less contention on a daily basis? Ask God to help you be a peacemaker whenever conflict arises during the next seven days.

CHAPTER 5

The Law of
THE SICKLE
The Power of Continuation

"Don't judge each day by the harvest you reap,
but by the seeds you plant."
– Robert Louis Stevenson

The parable of the sower is a simple description of God's plan for producing positive, lasting change in the lives of His people. The *sower* initiates change, the *seed* informs change, and the *soil* supports change. Then comes the *sickle.*

When anyone hears this charming analogy, he instinctively knows the story is moving toward the climactic day of harvest when the sower's labors will be rewarded. The word "harvest" can be used in multiple ways. It can refer to the time of reaping, the crop that was gathered, or the process of collecting valuable fruit. However one uses it, the word "harvest" always conveys the idea of results. Jesus used it to illustrate the outcome of thought and effort. The goal of sowing kingdom seed is salvation from sin and sanctification of the spirit. Or in simpler terms, it is about beneficial change: change in your spiritual condition and life circumstances.

The law of the sickle is the fourth law of success contained in the parable of the sower. It connects confidence in God's promises with belief in your power to exercise control over your life to produce desirable change. The behavioral term for this ability is *efficacy*. The biblical word is *faith*. Paul expressed the essence of this law when he proclaimed, "I can do all things through Christ who strengthens me" (Philippians 4:13).

The law of the sickle highlights three concepts critical to human success:

- Certainty of God's promise to us (*faith*); Hebrews 11:7
- Confidence in God's power within us (*fortitude*); Philippians 4:13
- Concentration on God's purpose before us (*focus*); John 13:31-35

Success and Growth

Some people are under the mistaken impression that spiritual fruit is produced effortlessly and instantaneously. No forethought or effort is required; just believe in Christ and *poof*! – transformation is immediate and comprehensive. This is hardly the case (James 1:21; 1 Corinthians 3:1-4). As with crops in the field, spiritual growth is typically so incremental that it is imperceptible at any given moment (Mark 4:26-29). As a result, Christian growth requires patience and diligence (1 Corinthians 9:27).

No doubt the seed contains its full potential from the moment it is planted, but intention and effort are necessary for fruit to come to maturity. Habits, attitudes and character are forged one painstaking choice at a time. The soul must be tended in the same way one cares for a garden. Unless soil is cultivated and seeds are nurtured, no plant can reach its full growth. For God's Word to take root, a humble heart is needed. For God's Word to produce fruit, a noble heart is essential. Deliberate weeding and watering are as important to godliness as to gardening. Unhelpful thoughts must be eliminated, and useful thoughts must be encouraged.

Growth Guaranteed

Christians can anticipate success when they prepare their hearts to hear and heed God's Word. Scripture is beneficial for strengthening relationships and accomplishing goals when the heart is ready to receive it. If met by faith, it aids personal growth, professional advancement and organizational success. Without faith, meaningful progress is limited and unsustainable.

Christ was the all-time champion of confident living. He knew that blessings are guaranteed to those who persevere in doing God's will. He also understood that suffering can be a forerunner of favorable things to come (James 1:2-3). Armed with this knowledge, Jesus endured the cross for the joy that was set before Him (Hebrews 12:2). Joyful living is the natural result of faithful living. It is confidence born of experience with God's Word. It is belief in the reliability of Scripture to produce positive ends.

Jesus never promised His followers excessive material wealth or limitless worldly pleasure, but He did guarantee His followers true riches and abundant life. The fruit of the Spirit is the "status symbol" of genuine success. Still, the fact that affluence and influence often follow increased wisdom and spirituality is hardly surprising (1 Kings 3:4-14). Insight and increase are frequent companions on the road to success.

Growth Balanced

When the seed is good and the soil is ready, success is certain as long as the sower stays focused on his business. How certain? One-hundred-percent, take-it-to-the-bank, God certain. Paul exhorted, "And let us not grow weary while doing good, for in due season we shall reap if we do not lose heart" (Galatians 6:9). To keep from losing heart, a sower must keep three things in mind:

- The *product* he desires (we shall reap)
- The *process* it requires (while doing good)
- The *promise* that inspires (in due season)

Balancing thought between these concepts is necessary for success. Daydreamers focus on the first and third but neglect the second. Two out of three will not do. Only by acting responsibly and industriously can you maximize your opportunities. The law of the sickle guarantees that if you sow seeds wisely and nurture them faithfully, the harvest will come. Or in other words, if you take care of your part, you can trust God to take care of His part. When you combine a clear purpose and a hopeful attitude with dogged persistence, incredible things happen.

The Product: Success and Goals

Success in any endeavor begins with knowing what you want. That is why goals are so valuable. The more specific your aims, the more powerful they become. Ill-defined goals are refined through thinking, speaking, writing and sharing. Through this process, clarity emerges to replace the hazy, unstructured emotions that well within your heart. The more precise and poignant your goals, the more forceful they become.

Envisioning a goal's completion produces emotional energy called drive. When you see and feel your dreams fulfilled, it provides the direction and motivation needed to transform them into reality. Potential becomes actual, and thoughts become things.

That does not mean God will do exactly what you want or expect in every situation. What you desire may not be reasonable or best. When you are displeased with your lot in life, anxiety will not improve your circumstances or outlook. What is needed is faith. You must trust that God will use the current situation to help you learn the lesson most needed at that moment. When you pay attention, self-improvement and progress are assured. Success and growth must be viewed from a soul perspective to appreciate their full value.

Some goals such as going to heaven and growing spiritually are common to all believers in Christ. Other goals are more personal in nature. In American culture, God grants you the right to make choices regarding profession, education, friendship, finances, health and recreation. From choosing your associates to choosing your address, the possibilities are limitless.

Although the ability to create a unique God-honoring life is available to all, few take this opportunity seriously. Most people do not tap the power of intention to make a masterpiece of their lives. The bulk of Earth's inhabitants timidly accept whatever comes their way rather than crafting the destiny of their dreams. They lack the courage required to withstand the dark forces of conformity. As a result, they downsize their dreams to avoid the pain of disappointment or disapproval. But yielding to life's pressures and others' expectations is a choice in itself.

Having praised the benefits of specific goals in developing a successful life, a qualification is now in order. Goals of this kind should be viewed as means rather than end. Their purpose is to motivate rather than dictate. Most goals should be held firmly but flexibly. A person lacking firmness will be double minded and unstable. But a person without flexibility will be crushed on the altar of obstinacy. For instance, Paul found that God altered his travel plans from time to time (Acts 16:6-10). Although he faced repeated roadblocks, he refused to give up. Had he stubbornly held to his itinerary, God would have been displeased. Had he quit out of frustration, God would have been dishonored. In the end Paul modified his route. He knew his private vision was not as crucial as his overarching mission. The details could change, but his devotion to God would not falter.

Likewise, Christians today should be unswerving in their commitment to live a faithful, loving, useful life. But when God overrules the particulars of your plan, it is wise to adapt. Do not abandon your dream. Refine it! Be creative rather than crushed. Keep praying and pressing on, and remember that your resourcefulness will be rewarded in due season.

God may be fine-tuning your plan or strengthening your character to face greater challenges in the future. Every lesson learned and obstacle surmounted becomes a stepping stone to a better life. When goals are growth-oriented, you can deal with anything that comes your way. Make your commitment to God's will greater than your own will (Matthew 26:39).

The Process: Success and Sweat

A farmer must not lose sight of the harvest he desires, but he cannot become so preoccupied with the future that he neglects today's opportunities. Without relinquishing his vision, he must move his focus to executing plans for procuring what he wants. Images of the day of reaping run in the background of his consciousness. Although ever present, those images are no longer the center of attention. Rather, they direct and sustain effort from behind the scenes. Awareness shifts to the steps for acquiring what is desired; making and implementing plans becomes the new priority. The mental spotlight is trained on the present rather than the future. This process includes eight essentials:

1. Accept responsibility.

One lesson learned from a garden is personal responsibility. A garden introduces you to yourself. It reflects your actions rather than your good intentions. Ralph Waldo Emerson wrote, "The sower may mistake and sow his peas crookedly; the peas make no mistake, but come up and show his line." Experience reveals your line.

Seldom does a stranger wander by and take it upon himself to weed and water your garden (although he might help himself to the fruits of your labor). In most cases, the garden in your backyard is what you alone make it. And most of your life experiences are similar. They are self-created. Your career, relationships, health, finances and character are primarily the result of choices you have made or failed to make over the course of a lifetime. They reveal who you are and what you have been thinking.

Even when circumstances are beyond your control, you still decide what to make of them. You choose your attitude – whether to suck it up or sulk. And you decide how to adapt – whether to dig in and redouble your efforts or whine and walk away. The crucial question is, "Which actions will produce the results I want?"

When people are more concerned with protecting their egos than producing better outcomes, their troubles persist. They prefer to fix blame rather than fix the problem. Denial, minimization and blame are the enemies of mental health and success because they distort reality and discourage initiative. Why work on a problem if it's *not* a problem (denial), it's not a *big* problem (minimization), or it's not *my* problem (blame)?

Maturity comes from accepting responsibility. Immaturity comes from evading responsibility. The successful adjust to life while the unsuccessful expect life to adjust to them. Wise people are willing to change. Foolish people would rather complain.

2. Test reality.

One of the keys to gardening is knowing what grows well in your climate, soil and environment. Cooperating with nature is more profitable than ignoring ecological facts. Trying to grow mountain laurel in the desert or orange groves in New England would be foolish and wasteful. Rhododendrons need shade, and citrus fruits need warmth.

Similarly, humans bloom and grow under different circumstances. Wise people spend time learning their gifts and passions to make the most of them. They also pay attention to the kind of environment that makes them feel fully alive. When people are out of their element, they may be marginally productive, but they will not be effective. Doing the wrong thing or laboring in the wrong environment is inefficient and unsatisfying. Greatness comes from getting in touch with who you were created to be and knowing the kind of atmosphere in which you thrive.

3. Review opportunities.
Much of life's frustration comes from failing to examine the full range of possibilities available to you. *Disappointment* occurs when you settle too soon for too little. Rest assured that life will seldom give you more than you ask. If you feel unworthy of the school, job, salary or relationship you desire, your mind will not give them full consideration because it wants to spare you pain. Although some things are beyond your reach, you can attain far more than you realize. Do not undersell yourself.

Despair occurs when you believe no desirable options are available. However, such hopelessness is seldom a reflection of reality. Rather, it results from the inability to see reasonable alternatives because of fear and discouragement. Just because your first option is unavailable does not mean that none is available. Choosing to be miserable because life will not conform to your wishes has more to do with lack of maturity than lack of opportunity.

4. Embrace risk.
Life is fraught with risks. Taking a shower places you at the scene of most household accidents. Driving to work exposes you to the possibility of a wreck. Eating out carries the potential for food poisoning. Getting married increases the likelihood of divorce. Obsessive attempts to eliminate all peril result in mental illness, social isolation and spiritual decline. Mental health requires the ability to distinguish between the *possibility* and *probability* of danger. Effective living requires the ability to take calculated risks.

All risks are not equal. There are stupid risks and smart risks; the difference between them is the degree of danger they entail. Danger can be assessed in three ways: frequency, duration and intensity. How often does something bad happen when engaging in this activity? Are the consequences long-term or short-term? And how severe is the potential suffering or loss? Conversely, what are the likely benefits of engaging in this particular behavior? Is the pleasure or profit worth the price? On this basis, you can differentiate between wise and foolish choices.

Flying commercially may be scary, but the safety record of the airline industry and the time savings are so huge that the risk is reasonable and minimal. Refusing to fly can limit career choices and professional advancement. It can also deprive you of valuable cultural experiences or time with family. Risking health or reputation for gratuitous pleasure or low-priority goals is reckless, but avoiding all risk is faithless.

A successful life requires assessing and accepting reasonable risk. It is a life marked by pluck and persistence. Foolish people engage in indiscriminate risk or evasion of all risk. Intelligent people are selective risk takers. Inaction is not an option, and indecision is not a virtue. They begin cautiously, but when they commit to a course of action, they undertake it fearlessly. They are choosy but courageous, prudent but daring.

5. Seek assistance.

The reason most people do not get what they want in life is because they do not ask (James 4:2). In other words, the breakdown is on their end rather than God's. The goal is attainable and God's help is accessible, but they fail to take advantage of the resources at their disposal. They are too insecure to request help in their time of need (Hebrews 4:16).

God's provision usually comes in the form of a person who can provide the knowledge, means, encouragement or accountability necessary to succeed. But the downcast eyes of the discouraged never behold the blessings available for the asking. Their lack of progress is because of their outlook rather than insurmountable obstacles.

Successful people are good at asking for help. They are free of the illusion of the self-made man. They do not ask others to do what they should do, but they do not hesitate to seek assistance when needed. Because they are humble and grateful, people enjoy helping them. Ask yourself, "Do I enjoy giving directions, advice or assistance to someone who is truly in need and appreciative of my aid?" No one likes to be used or conned, but wanting to help others is human nature. So why not bless others (and yourself) by giving them an opportunity to do what God created them to do?

6. Refuse distractions.

Fruitful people know how to focus. They have developed the ability to say no to diversions and concentrate on things they can control. When circumstances are beyond their control, they accept them as facts of life (at least for the present) and adapt to them as best they can. For example, complaining about traffic wastes time and energy. How much better is it to adjust to reality than rail against it? You could change jobs, adjust your commute time, carpool, take public transportation, enjoy your favorite music, or listen to educational material. Sometimes the answer is to adjust your attitude. Count your blessings, and refuse to be drawn into discontent. Remind yourself how wonderful it is to have a car and a job. When you catch yourself becoming grouchy, it is a sign that your mind took a wrong turn somewhere.

Another major distraction is overcommitment. A person is overcommitted when he takes on more than is feasible or desirable. It occurs when obligation exceeds capacity or agreements compromise priorities. Saying yes to too many good things is the main barrier to accomplishing great things. Some diversions are immoral and unhealthy. Others are harmless but worthless. However, the sneakiest kind of distraction is a beneficial activity that is not the best use of your time. For example, a mother can get so busy cleaning house that she forgets to play with her children. Or a church elder can sit in so many meetings that he finds little time to spend with people. Doing good can be bad when it keeps you from fulfilling a higher purpose. Learn to say no and let go in order to grow. Less becomes more when it allows you to honor your highest priorities and pursue excellence.

7. Check progress.

Wavering and vacillating are not admirable behaviors, but reflection and redirection are highly commendable. Assess your progress and adjust your plans on a regular basis. By monitoring your movement and modifying your methods, you engage life realistically. When values are not in question, success is a practical results-oriented business. Holding inflexibly to outdated tactics or obsolete methods is not perseverance; it is pigheadedness. Change the means, but keep your dreams. Reframing "failure" is something resilient people do well. They leverage rather than internalize it. They view it as experience instead of misfortune. The same situation that mires one person in discouragement inspires another to take new action, and disposition usually accounts for the difference. A fear-based life yields doubt. A faith-based life produces determination. Courage and timidity are more about attitude than circumstance.

8. Resolve to finish.

Successful people are finishers. They do not leave a trail of broken promises and unfinished tasks behind them. They complete what they start and tie up loose ends. The ability to see things to completion makes people invaluable in a self-centered world. Discipline turns dreams into "done." Just think about all the worthwhile things you have accomplished in your lifetime. In every case was a degree of difficulty that challenged your resolve. The pride of achievement was in direct proportion to the challenges you overcame.

Staying on task is critical to success in any endeavor; it is the sister of initiative in the family of success. In the family of failure, however, quitting and procrastination are like twins separated at birth. One comes at the beginning of a project and the other toward the end. Yet they are mirror images of each other separated only by time. When a job is unpleasant, attention and energy shift to more enjoyable things. Dodging duty can occur in the beginning or toward the end. In either case, such behavior is fatal to the accomplishment of worthwhile goals. To be successful you must be steadfast (1 Corinthians 15:58).

The key to resolve is not sheer willpower but dream power. A captivating vision draws hearts unto it. The likelihood that you will finish what you start is increased by the number and strength of reasons you have for reaching completion. Dreams are not only compelling but propelling.

This is where thought control enters the picture (2 Corinthians 10:3-5). Tenacity is a byproduct of focused thinking. Unsuccessful people have undisciplined minds. Their thoughts tend to drift and fluctuate (James 1:5-8; Ephesians 4:14). Successful people have disciplined minds. Through practice they have learned how to channel their thoughts in useful directions and keep their minds on track.

The Promise: Success and Confidence

To encourage the Galatians to maintain a life of good works, Paul told them about a promise God gave to sustain their efforts (Galatians 6:9). God guaranteed that those who sow to the Spirit will succeed if they do not give up. Everyone experiences moments of physical and emotional fatigue, but those who press on will discover they were nearer their dreams than they ever imagined. What do you do when you feel faint, when you sense you are at the end of your reserves, when exhaustion stares you in the eye? Such moments exist in every meaningful undertaking:

- **Moses** faced it in the wilderness before he led Israel to the Promised Land.

- **Paul** faced it at Troas before he carried the gospel into Europe.

- **Mark** faced it at Perga before he became a successful evangelist and writer.

- **Peter** faced it in the courtyard before he converted 3,000 on Pentecost.

- **John** faced it on Patmos before he completed the book of Revelation.

- **Jesus** faced it in Gethsemane before He was resurrected and glorified.

Before you throw in the towel, ask yourself, "Do I really want to question God's trustworthiness? He promised that, in due season, I will reap if I faint not." To faint means to grow tired or dispirited and give up. As long as you are faithful, a wonderful harvest awaits. You are not guaranteed what you wish for, but you are guaranteed what you sow because everything brings forth after its kind.

The key to utilizing the law of the sickle is to understand the phrase "in due season." Success is a process that entails the investment of time and energy. Few victories occur without patience and perseverance. I must be willing to *work for* and *wait for* what I *wish for*.

People who are lazy and impatient are doomed to a life of continual disappointment. Instant gratification and overnight success are hardly the foundations of a fruitful life.

- Career goals require apprenticeship, certification or advanced degrees.
- Financial goals hinge on spending less and saving more.
- Health goals require sleep, exercise and good nutrition.
- Relational goals call for less selfishness and more togetherness.
- Spiritual goals demand patience, practice and prayer.

The farmer's harvest does not follow the day of planting (James 5:7-11). Neither do meaningful goals happen instantly or easily. There is a natural timing for growing plants, healing bones, accruing wealth, shedding weight, building trust or forging character (Ecclesiastes 2:1-8). As a result, few shortcuts are found along the path to success.

Resolve is the final puzzle piece for completing the picture of enduring success. But what is the source of steadfastness? It is a quality of soul born of certainty. Vacillation is the child of doubt; determination is the child of faith. Nothing sustains effort like confidence in the reliability of God and His Word.

The law of the sickle says, "If I prepare wisely, sow bountifully and nurture consistently, a matching harvest is assured." On the other hand, the quickest and surest way to fail is to give up. There is no shortage of reasons to quit, but do not yield to the temptation. You will not like the results. Continue the struggle with this in mind: Only one ultimate goal really exists in life, and that is to magnify God (Philippians 1:20). Trust Him, love Him, worship Him and serve Him to the end. This is glory and victory.

Section Review

- Information is necessary for transformation (Romans 12:2).
- The best information for positive change is found in God's Word (John 8:32).
- The ability of information to work depends on your heart (Proverbs 4:23).
- Potential is realized by making well-informed choices and sticking with them (Joshua 24:15).

Questions

1. What idea does the word "harvest" convey?

2. If spiritual growth is not instantaneous or easy, how does it occur?

3. What two things does Christian growth require?

4. How do people avoid disappointment in regard to their goals?

5. What is the status symbol of genuine success?

6. Name three things a person can think about to keep from losing heart.

7. Name four ways that ill-defined goals are refined.

8. How should goals be held?

9. Successful people are good at asking for what?

10. How can a person increase the likelihood of finishing what he starts?

Discussion Questions

1. How can a garden introduce you to yourself?

2. How is experience a composite of your past choices?

3. How do you get in touch with the person you were created to be?

Assignment

Seed of the Week: Kindness

When and where will you sow a small seed of kindness this week? Tiny acts of thoughtfulness combine to make the world a wonderful place. Stop waiting on a chance for a newsworthy display of humanitarianism. Just do a good turn today.

Weed of the Week: Spitefulness

It is easy to get caught up in a tit-for-tat-battle of wounded egos. When you feel an urge to get even, get out your hoe: A weed is sprouting in the garden of your mind.

Reflection and Prayer:

What do you reap when you sow more kindness and less spite on a daily basis? Ask God to help you be more considerate and less cruel during the next seven days.

The SOILS

In gardening, good soil supports the growth of seed. In Christianity, a good heart supports the growth of the spirit. Humility softens the heart to make it teachable. Honor strengthens the heart to make it noble. A heart that is meek and principled provides a healthy environment for spiritual development.

What make a heart good are its patterns of thought. The first three soils in Jesus' parable describe ineffective ways of thinking. When your thoughts degrade, discourage or distract you, they run counter to your interests. Thoughts that oppose your goals or debase your soul must be eliminated. You cannot get the most out of your life without getting lesser thoughts out of your mind.

- Wayside thoughts squander my potential and keep me from *beginning*.

- Rocky thoughts weaken my commitment and keep me from *finishing*.

- Thorny thoughts dilute my dreams and keep me from *succeeding*.

The secret to success is paying attention to the things that matter. It is learning to make choices consistent with your goals. It is remembering what you want and why you want it. It is holy initiative and prayerful persistence.

The key is to hold the best possible thoughts in your mind. The more you cultivate this ability, the more you can leverage the Seed Principle to produce a harvest of blessings. A disciplined mind is a fruitful mind.

Your life today is the residue of your past thinking. To improve your life you must improve your thoughts. The more honest, loving and hopeful your thoughts are, the more successful you will be. In the next four chapters, you will learn how to turn your heart into rich soil for spiritual growth. By developing a better way of thinking, you will develop a better way of life.

> *"Keep your heart with all diligence, for out of it*
> *spring the issues of life."*
> *(Proverbs 4:23)*

CHAPTER 6

Hard GROUND

How Broken Is Your Spirit?

*"Though the land be good, you cannot have
an abundant crop without cultivation."*
– Plato

Christianity is about your heart – its purity and productivity. Jesus wants to put something holy in your heart that will bless you in increasing measure. As it grows, you will grow in happiness and effectiveness. That gift is the seed of the kingdom.

Satan wants to remove what is holy from your heart. And if he cannot remove it, he hopes to restrict it so it will never bear fruit. The outcome of this battle between heaven and hell will be decided by you. Will you prize the gift of the gospel and cherish its benefits for your relationships, career and destiny? Or will you underestimate the evil one's determination to rob you of this resource for producing fullness of life?

To help us guard against this loss, Jesus drew on his hearers' familiarity with first-century farming to illustrate the way different people respond to His teaching. A life well lived is the natural consequence of hearing and heeding His words. An unfruitful life is the result of disregarding His life-changing message. When Scripture is embraced, the future becomes larger and brighter; when rejected, the prospects for tomorrow are predictably bleak. For good or ill, your heart is the frontline in the struggle for abundant life.

Packed Soil

In the parable of the sower, seed fell on four distinct kinds of soil. The first was wayside soil – the hardened path along the edge of a field or seed plot packed down by people coming and going. As individuals go about their business in life, they sometimes step on each other's hearts. A broken promise here, a careless word there, and the spirit begins to lose its tenderness. Some injuries are intentional, others are inadvertent. Regardless of the motive, the soul's scars accumulate and the heart grows harder one disappointment at a time. In her introduction to Victor Hugo's novel *Ninety-Three*, Ayn Rand wrote,

> When people look back on their childhood or youth, their wistfulness comes from the memory, not of what their lives had been in those years, but of what life had then promised to be. The expectation of some indefinable splendor, of the unusual, the exciting, the great, is an attribute of youth – and the process of aging is the process of that expectation's gradual extinction. One does not have to let that happen. But that fire dies for lack of fuel, under the gray weight of disappointments.

Wounds, worldliness, and the weight of life's cares can compact the heart and sear the conscience (Romans 2:5; 1 Timothy 4:1-2). To keep from hurting, some choose to quit caring. They stop believing in themselves and others (1 Corinthians 13:7). But the pain of callousness exceeds the old ache of humanness.

The trampled heart is a sad specimen but not a hopeless one. Cynics and sinners can revive their consciences by embracing pain previously avoided. That means re-encountering the Word and facing its message. The twinge of truth is preferable to the sting of sin. Repentance relieves godly sorrow and allows deadened hearts to live again.

Plentiful Problems

Was the sower's seed intended for the cement-like surface of the wayside? Planting seed on this toughened terrain makes as little sense as gardening on an asphalt highway. Agriculturally speaking, it fell there as the sower broadcast handfuls of seed attempting to reach every corner of useful ground. Spiritually speaking, it illustrates that

God wants all men to be saved and come to a knowledge of the truth (1 Timothy 2:3-4). But the question remains, "What will come of this environmentally challenged seed?"

Several factors made it unlikely that the wayside soil would produce anything of value. The main problem was that the ground was not tilled or prepared to receive the seed. Without a loose covering of soil for protection, the seed lay exposed on the surface. It could easily be washed away by rain with no root to hold it in place. If it did germinate, it would hardly sprout before a passerby would crush it underfoot. Yet the most ominous threat was predators. Birds would feast upon the seed as though it were a banquet specially prepared for their enjoyment. This small band of thieves would devour the seed before it could ever develop.

Spiritual Seed

Jesus took His disciples aside and explained the deeper meaning of His parable. The seed stood for the Word of God, and the soil represented the heart of man (Mark 4:14). Words are seeds because they effect change, generate fruit or produce outcomes. That is their purpose and value.

The sower's seed is called the Word of God because it proceeds from Him and possesses the unique properties of a divine message (Luke 8:11). Theologians stress the special qualities of God's Word by calling it inspired, inerrant and authoritative. A more practical person will simply say, "It is true." The aforementioned theological terms are merely ways of emphasizing the reliability of God's Word. Because it is God-breathed (inspired), it is eternally true. Because it is flawless (inerrant), it is entirely true. Because it works (is authoritative), it is effectually true. Yet when all is said and done, it is simply true.

The Bible is powerful because every instruction corresponds with the realities of life. The Word is true both factually and functionally. That is to say, it is not only accurate but effective (Isaiah 55:10-11). The Bible makes you a better person when you obey its teachings (Romans 12:2). Simply put, it works.

Kingdom Seed

Matthew referred to God's Word as the seed of the "kingdom" (Matthew 13:19). That means whenever you obey Jesus' teaching, you demonstrate that He rules your life. And the more you heed Christ's words, the more heaven comes to earth. His kingdom advances one faithful decision at a time.

God's initial commands to sinners include belief, repentance, confession and baptism. These hold a special priority without which further obedience becomes meaningless. Each of these directives represents a guiding principle without which life cannot be lived effectively. To live successfully, four convictions must be planted deep within the heart:

- **Faith**: A successful life requires well-placed trust.
  Believe that Jesus is God's Son and the Lord and Savior of mankind.

- **Repentance**: A successful life requires personal responsibility.
  Quit blaming others for the parts of your life that aren't working, and start changing.

- **Confession**: A successful life requires absolute honesty.
  Acknowledge your inadequacy and Christ's sufficiency.

- **Baptism**: A successful life requires willing sacrifice.
  Give up your old life to begin enjoying new life.

The Sower's Adversary

After the sower distributed his seed, one appeared on the scene who was unwilling to let God's Word have its full effect. This formidable enemy was described in three ways. He was called:

1. **Wicked** (Matthew 13:19) because his conduct was detrimental rather than beneficial.

2. **Satan** (Mark 4:15) because his behavior was adversarial rather than friendly.

3. **Devil** (Luke 8:12) because his methods were duplicitous rather than aboveboard.

The terms depicting the evil one demonstrate that his actions were not innocent and harmless but intentional and evil.

Jesus compared Satan to a hungry bird that takes away seed lying exposed on an uncultivated path, a sad scene of wasted potential. The seed, so full of life and possibility, would never sprout or root or bear fruit. And that is precisely what the wicked one intended. By removing the Word from a person's life, the devil eliminates the catalyst for positive change and growth. You must think differently to live differently. The alternative is stagnation and conformation. Without the benefit of God's Word, you are stuck in sin and cannot move forward in life.

The Need for Speed

Jesus used two dramatic words to show how speedily Satan undertook his work. Mark says he came *immediately* to take away the Word (Mark 4:14-15). Matthew added that he *snatched away* what was sown (Matthew 13:19). Obviously, Satan understood that time was of the essence. So what was the big hurry? It is much easier for a bird to swoop down and scoop up a watermelon seed than a full-grown watermelon. Once the seed roots and begins to grow, the enemy's work gets harder. It is always easier to stop something in the beginning rather than after it is under way. Satan has many strategies he can employ to confuse people's minds and discourage their hearts, but nothing succeeds like stealing the seed before it ever takes hold.

When the Word is misunderstood or unappreciated, it will be ignored or rejected (Romans 1:21). One who does not value the Word is unlikely to obey it. The implication is that this ignorance is willful and blameworthy. Like seed that cannot penetrate a hardened path, God's Word cannot break through a hardened heart. Mere exposure to the Bible is not enough. You must meditate on its meaning and contemplate how it can be applied to your life. When you fail to embrace the Word and act upon it, it leaves your awareness and lesser thoughts quickly take its place. To keep important ideas from getting away, you must do something with them. You could:

1. Capture them in writing.

2. Determine the next faithful step.

3. Commit to take action within three days.

Taking any constructive step reinforces the thought and builds momentum for doing more. Failure to act within a reasonable time frame indicates you probably never will. Quit kidding yourself, and get busy.

Seed and Salvation

To thwart the seed-stealer, you must cultivate a deep desire for the seed of the kingdom. James says, "Receive with meekness the implanted word, which is able to save your souls" (James 1:21). A know-it-all lacks the requisite meekness to accept spiritual direction. Humility loosens the soil of the spirit and prepares the heart to receive the soul-saving Word. So the prophet urged, "Break up your fallow [uncultivated] ground, for it is time to seek the Lord" (Hosea 10:12).

The connection between the Word and salvation explains the motive behind Satan's swift action (Luke 8:12). The Word must be removed as quickly as possible "lest they should believe and be saved." Salvation is linked to the Word through belief, or as John put it, "And you shall know the truth, and the truth shall make you free" (John 8:32). Liberation from mistaken beliefs and their harmful consequences comes from uprooting them and replacing them with beliefs that produce beneficial results. Rescue cannot be accomplished apart from renewing the mind. James explained, "Of His own will He brought us forth *by the word of truth*, that we might be a kind of firstfruits of His creatures" (James 1:18). Apart from the seed of God's Word, salvation is impossible.

A fruitful life requires a humble, teachable spirit to gain new knowledge that makes fresh growth possible. Whether the growth one seeks is spiritual, professional or relational, the principle is the same. An attitude of openness and receptivity to truth is critical for success in any worthwhile endeavor.

Tilling for Truth

Hearts grow hard as people lose interest in truth. "To harden is to take from a man the sense of the true, the just, and even the useful, so that he is no longer open to the wise admonitions and significant circumstances which should turn him aside from the evil way on which he has entered" (David Lipscomb and J.W. Shepherd, *Gospel Advocate New Testament Commentaries*, Romans, Vol. 6, p. 176). Some are oblivious to truth. Others are hostile to truth. Either way, they are self-satisfied and content to a fault. They do not hunger and thirst for righteousness or seek first the kingdom of God. To protect their egos and agendas, they close themselves off from information that could help them but would change them.

Their hearts are like sun-baked earth. Seed cannot enter, and potential cannot emerge. They are trapped in one frame of mind, unaware of the forces shaping and limiting their thoughts. Christ calls them out of their comfort zones and into life's challenge zone. His teaching can renovate and elevate their thinking if only they will let it (Luke 13:34). Jesus employed several images to describe people who undervalue truth and prefer comfort to growth. He compared them to brittle wineskins that would rupture if filled with new wine (Matthew 9:17). And He likened them to cloth that would tear if patched with new material (v. 16). People whose minds will not stretch are in grave danger. Old wineskins, well-worn cloth and wayside ground all illustrate the same peril: the danger of inflexible thinking. Abundant life does not require a high IQ, but it does demand that a person be willing to think.

When people will not consider new ideas, their hearts are like untilled earth. Information cannot penetrate their defenses. As a result, they cannot see imminent threats or appreciate timely opportunities. They prefer fantasy to reality and comforting lies to hard truth. They have one-track minds on the road to ruin.

Persistent personal and relational problems indicate that little real thinking is taking place. When people ignore or oppose beneficial ideas, they are stuck in denial. Because they do not consider the full range of possibilities available to them, they repeat the desperate and dysfunctional behaviors of the past. Problems are a call for new thinking. Patterns of conflict, anger or depression result from failing to think creatively and effectively. Fear, worry, cruelty, divorce, crime and suicide all occur for want of a better thought.

Spiritual Plows

Questions are like plows that cultivate the mind to break up assumptions and prejudices. To live spiritually is to ask questions, not for curiosity's sake but to engage life more responsibly. Without questions, people make ignorant judgments rather than informed decisions.

Spiritual minds are inquiring minds. Successful people listen actively and think deeply. That is why Jesus' favorite teaching methods included thought-provoking questions, stories and statements. Look at the verses below, and consider how Jesus engaged people and drew them into the learning process:

- "For what profit is it to a man if he gains the whole world, and loses his own soul? Or what will a man give in exchange for his soul?" (Matthew 16:26).

- "So which of these three do you think was neighbor to him who fell among the thieves?" (Luke 10:36).

- "Therefore, whatever you want men to do to you, do also to them, for this is the Law and the Prophets" (Matthew 7:12).

- "He who is without sin among you, let him throw a stone at her first" (John 8:7).

- "What is written in the law? What is your reading of it?" (Luke 10:26).

Thought Leaders

When Jesus established His church, He provided qualifications for its leaders that stressed the importance of mental alertness and agility (1 Timothy 3:1-7). Elders are temperate people who do not let their emotions override their judgment. They are sober-minded and bring all their faculties to bear on issues facing the church.

Leaders also model spiritual thinking for those they serve. They consider others' needs and not just their own. They look to the future and not just the present. They examine problems from multiple angles rather than through a single lens. Those who observe how they reason can grow by following their example.

Narrow, selfish, reflexive thinking disqualifies a person from leadership in God's kingdom. According to Paul, people who are quarrelsome, violent, greedy or preoccupied with alcohol are not prepared to lead others. Their behavior reveals an underdeveloped thought process. Spiritual-mindedness is mature thinking informed by Scripture. It is what happens when God's Word dwells in you richly (Colossians 3:16).

Value Differences

Insecure people see others' viewpoints as threatening. Secure people know most disagreements are based on simple differences of opinion. For example, Paul and Barnabas parted company when they could not agree on the details of a second mission trip (Acts 15:36-40). The sticking point was whether to take John Mark, who left the work at Perga. Both valued Mark and the mission, but each had different priorities. Paul's goal was to reach as many lost people as possible during the upcoming journey. Barnabas was intent on recovering the man before him, believing he would extend their labors long after their lifetimes. Both viewpoints were valid.

How we think about differences matters. Hasty judgments are seldom helpful (Matthew 7:1-5). Pause to ask what a person is seeing that you may not see. What is he valuing that you do not value? What can you learn from him and appreciate about his perspective? Asking these questions allows you to respect others even when you differ with them. The tendency to interpret all differences self-righteously is a sign of closed-mindedness. So be careful. There may be a difference between what you know and what you think you know.

Humble and Hungry

People with honest, open hearts live fruitful lives. People with hard hearts live comparatively barren lives. If you are hiding from the truth about yourself, your mind will explain away your responsibility for the consequences your choices have created. When that happens, even the best question will have trouble breaking through the barriers you have constructed to evade reality.

In farming, a plow does its best work in good soil. In personal growth, a question is most effective when someone is spiritually sensitive and eager to learn and improve. When people are humble and hungry for truth, the desire of their hearts will be granted (Matthew 5:6).

Fruitful lives are the result of listening intently, thinking honestly and choosing wisely. Abundant life is what you get when you live with your heart, mind and eyes wide open. Or as God expressed it, "You will seek Me and find Me, when you search for Me with all your heart" (Jeremiah 29:13).

Questions

1. How many types of soil are mentioned in Jesus' parable?

2. What is the literal meaning of "wayside"?

3. What does the "wayside" figuratively represent?

4. What does the seed stand for in this story?

5. What happened to the seed that fell by the wayside?

6. Why is wayside soil unproductive?

7. Who do the birds represent?

8. What three words are used to describe the evil one?

9. How quickly did Satan come to take away the Word?

10. Why did Satan snatch away the Word?

Discussion Questions

1. How are hearts like trampled paths?

2. In what ways are words like seeds?

3. How can you keep your heart tender?

Assignment

Seed of the Week: Goodness

When and where will you sow a small seed of goodness this week? Goodness is doing what you were designed to do. Because Christians were created for good works (Ephesians 2:10), how will you make yourself a blessing today?

Weed of the Week: Hurtfulness

When you feel like doing something hurtful to someone, resist the temptation by fast-forwarding to the future. Imagine how you will feel when you look back on the choice later. Although weed seeds seem harmless, mature weeds are always detrimental and a source of regret.

Reflection and Prayer:

What do you reap when you sow more good and less harm on a daily basis? Ask God to help you be more helpful and less hurtful this week.

CHAPTER 7

Rocky
GROUND
How Deep Is Your Love?

"One for the rock, One for the crow,
One to die, And one to grow."
– Old English saying

Soil conditioning is the key to successful gardening and landscaping. When preparing plant beds, it is wise to remove unwanted rocks and roots and add organic matter that lightens heavy soils and helps them to breathe. Additives such as peat moss, aged wood chips and sand improve the soil. Organic matter such as lawn clippings and leaves can hold water without compacting roots. Preparation of this kind pays off as plants thrive in a superb environment.

But just as plants need healthy surroundings for optimum growth, so humans require the right conditions to become the best people they can be. Caring families, faithful friends and loving churches are rich soil for human growth. Yet outward circumstances have less bearing on your development than the inward state of your heart. Soul conditioning is the most important factor in successful living. Therefore, spiritual gardeners eagerly devote themselves to cultivating their innermost beings. Worldly obstructions must be removed; spiritual substance must be added. A sin-reduced, love-enriched heart is the ideal setting for the soul to flourish.

As Jesus continued His farming analogy, He introduced a second type of soil to depict the danger of an inadequate response to His teaching. In the first image the ground was never turned. This time the ground was tilled, but ledges of stone lurked just beneath the surface. Readers are moved from a picture of a man who is hard-hearted to one who is half-hearted, and the result is equally disappointing. In the first scenario the gospel was neglected or rejected altogether. In the second it received enthusiastic but superficial obedience. In both cases God was displeased by the absence of fruit (John 15:1-2). Where faith is genuine, the Word is productive. Therefore, unfruitful lives are a sign of dead faith.

Fast Times

In contrast to wayside soil that cannot be penetrated, rocky soil receives the seed without delay. Growth begins immediately but is short-lived. The problem can be viewed from two angles: limited room or limiting rock. In other words, attention can be focused on the lack of resources (insufficient earth) or the reason they are in short supply (impeding rock).

Jesus began by stressing the impressive start of the seed. When received by the soil, it germinated right away and the young plant nearly jumped out of the ground. The pace of growth made the plant's future appear promising, but in the end, it would prove problematic. Beginning something, however remarkable the start, is not the same as finishing (1 Corinthians 10:1-5). Those captivated with the Christian life eventually will be asked to pay the price of a life of faith.

In Jesus' parable the surface soil contained all the resources necessary to jump-start the seed, yet sustained growth required a different environment. A womb is sufficient for a fetus but not a first-grader. A cradle is suitable for an infant but not an adolescent. Living things need room to grow. A confining atmosphere can stunt growth or stop it altogether (Mark 2:22). Oppressive environments that focus on controlling people rather than unleashing their potential cannot sustain growth over the long haul.

Happy Times

The gospel produces intense emotions in those who receive the seed of the kingdom, and the most common reaction is immense joy (Mark 4:16). Two conversion stories from the book of Acts illustrate this point:

• **The Ethiopian Eunuch** (Acts 8:38-39): "So he commanded the chariot to stand still. And both Philip and the eunuch went down into the water, and he baptized him. Now when they came up out of the water, the Spirit of the Lord caught Philip away, so that the eunuch saw him no more; and he went on his way *rejoicing*."

• **The Philippian Jailor** (Acts 16:33-34): "And he took them the same hour of the night and washed their stripes. And immediately he and all his family were baptized. Now when he had brought them into his house, he set food before them; and he *rejoiced*, having believed in God with all his household."

Being able to sense that you are forgiven, at peace with God and heaven-bound is the greatest feeling in the world.

The gospel has a similar effect on those who view the development of a new Christian. Just as parents delight in charting a child's physical growth, church families take pleasure in noting the spiritual progress of new converts. Christian maturity is marked by character and contribution. Virtuous living, faithful assembling, cheerful giving and joyful serving are all earmarks of spiritual advancement.

Witnessing healthy growth is pleasurable, but especially when the observer assisted in the process. When plants or people or projects live up to their potential, it is enjoyable to watch. Yet it is even more exciting for the manager, mentor or master gardener who encouraged the development.

The hometown crowd gets excited by the success of its beloved team, but their joy cannot compete with the satisfaction of the coach. Fans follow the exploits of an admired player, but their satisfaction cannot compare with the pride of the athlete's mom and dad. Few things are as satisfying as contributing to someone's growth, and the pleasure is multiplied when improvement occurs in the spiritual arena.

Hot Times

Conversely, nothing is as disappointing as watching a cherished dream go up in smoke or seeing a loved one slowly self-destruct. In Jesus' parable, the trouble began when the sun reached its peak and turned up the temperature on the tender plant. The problem was not a prolonged drought or excessively high heat. Jesus described an average sunny day with the normal stress that all growing things must endure. The difficulty was not with the seed or sower or sun; the problem was with the soil.

When the sun reached its highest point, the plant's shoots hunted for revitalizing moisture. Their search ended in futility because no water was accessible to replenish them. The roots were not long enough or strong enough to achieve their aim. Rather than renewal, the plant experienced ruin.

Underdeveloped roots are a problem for people as well as plants. The job of a root is to stabilize a plant and supply its need for food and water. As growing things get bigger, their needs increase. To satisfy their hunger and thirst, their roots must extend their reach. The sun makes plants grow by causing them to seek out available resources. When people do not stretch their minds or reach beyond familiar experiences, they fail to grow as God intended. Small-minded people suffer from undersized roots. Great souls are characterized by spiritual depth and breadth.

"Scorched" is the term Jesus used to describe the plant's deprived condition (Mark 4:6). It denotes the onset of surface damage to the plant's natural color and texture. These signs of distress clearly indicate danger, and yet a scorched plant is not destined to die. If the right steps are taken in a timely manner, the injury can be contained. However, if appropriate action is not undertaken, the plant will wither. To "wither away" describes a gradual process of decline. If symptoms are not relieved, the end result is death.

Something similar happens when souls are deprived of the refreshing power of faith, hope and love – the moisture of the soul. Without access to God's renewing Word, spirits become parched and eventually succumb. But as long as souls maintain contact with Christ, they can bear any difficulty known to man (1 Corinthians 10:13; Philippians 4:13). In fact, trials can be incredible growth opportunities (James 1:2-4). Adversity does not have to be dreaded and avoided at all costs. Daily challenges can be expected and embraced in faith (Romans 8:28). The key to success is deeper spiritual roots that refresh the soul in times of stress.

Hard Times

When people come across information with the potential to change life for the better, some hearts operate like stony ground. The seed or idea is not rejected, but neither is it wholly embraced. Hearers lack the depth of thought and commitment needed to see it through to completion. Because the Word never goes deep, it does not touch who they really are.

Rocks are faulty beliefs and harmful attitudes that limit the influence of spiritual ideas. The problem is not with the initial reception of Jesus' teaching. In fact, that occurs almost too easily. There is no hesitation when the information is first encountered. But if new ideas are accepted too quickly, they may be discarded with equal speed. It is not uncommon for a person to make a commitment without thinking about all that it entails. Jesus warned against making precipitous promises and repeatedly urged would-be followers to count the cost of genuine discipleship (Luke 14:25-35; Matthew 8:19-20).

Costly Times

Career

Every important choice in life involves a cost. When you choose a career, for instance, you must think about the pitfalls as well as the perks. Being a doctor pays well, but it also requires long hours at work and lots of time on call. Being a teacher is highly rewarding, but the pay is modest and parents can be difficult at times. People are more likely to be satisfied and stick with their chosen profession if they go into it with their eyes wide open.

Companions

Careful consideration also should be given to selecting companions. No one can do you more harm or good than your spouse or best friend. These are the people you spend most of your time with and, therefore, are the ones to whom you are most vulnerable. When choosing a mate, wise people look for good character as well as good looks. Bad traits minimized during dating become more important once the honeymoon is over. Divorce statistics prove that one can "fall out of love" as quickly as falling into it.

Romance has its place, but infatuation is a shaky foundation for building a family. When emotional highs fade, the responsibilities of life grow larger with each passing day. That is why discernment is crucial for choosing your closest allies. Satisfying relationships are seldom the product of wishful thinking.

Conversion

Matters of religion also deserve serious deliberation. The price tag of spiritual devotion is high, and failure to consider the cost can leave a person unprepared to keep the faith. Examine the truthfulness of tenets and not just their appeal. Consider the duties of discipleship as well as the benefits of church membership. True conversion involves conviction and commitment, not convenience and comfort.

Choices based on unexamined ideas do not hold up over time. To establish lasting commitments, you must go deeper. Half-heartedness simply will not do. In a divided heart, delight can turn to disgust and love to loathing in a single sunny day. Stress puts your choices to the test, and loosely held beliefs cannot bear up under the strain of life.

Peaceful Times

No doubt, the gospel has incredible power to produce joy (Matthew 13:20; Luke 15:10; 1 Thessalonians 2:19). The angels announced that fact the moment Christ entered the world: "Do not be afraid, for behold, I bring you good tidings of great joy which will be to all people. For there is born to you this day in the city of David a Savior, who is Christ the Lord" (Luke 2:10).

The joy effect is seen in many conversion stories from the book of Acts. The joy of being forgiven follows the joy of learning that forgiveness is possible. Hearing the gospel produces hope and anticipation; obeying the gospel provides healing and appreciation. What a relief when the burden of sin has been lifted. Guilt vanishes, and gratitude takes its place. The elation is almost indescribable.

Troublesome Times

But a dramatic shift occurs with the onset of trouble. A brief look at the ministries of Jesus and His apostles shows that Christian living is not devoid of difficulties. Jesus' teaching will improve your life, but

He never promised an easy life. A successful life is one of character and contribution, not idleness and indulgence. It is one of service rather than self-centeredness and of sanctification rather than sensuality. Just as surely as the sun rises, your beliefs and values will undergo daily testing. Like a plant under the noonday sun, your convictions will be challenged by tribulation, persecution and temptation (Matthew 13:21; Mark 4:17; Luke 8:13). Whether commitments are feigned or genuine becomes evident in hard times. Beliefs are not authenticated by what you profess but by what you practice (James 2:18). And they are most clearly seen in times of intense pressure. The heart is laid bare in the heat of battle between courageous and cowardly choices. That is why character shines brightest in its darkest hour.

"Beliefs" are a sham when behavior contradicts them. When hypocrisy is exposed, people claim their misconduct was due to special circumstances. Consider this example from everyday life. Workers who repeatedly show up late to work have no shortage of justifications for their tardiness: "My spouse turned off the alarm clock" or "There was a wreck on the interstate" or "My car wouldn't start." When excuse-ridden behavior becomes a pattern, it interferes with accountability and corrective action. Playing the blame game reduces efficiency and lowers self-esteem. Deep down, underachievers know they are being dishonest. Excuses are strongholds of stubbornness guarded by self-deception (Jeremiah 17:9).

When work performance is marked by delay and disorganization, people like to blame their busy schedules. Only the most naïve are fooled by this ruse. The trouble is seldom with insufficient time or impossible work demands. The problem is usually a lack of character. Integrity was never rooted deep enough to sustain punctuality, productivity and personal responsibility. In the parable of the sower, Jesus showed that the reason for the withering plant did not rest with extenuating circumstances. The problem was not the sun but the soil. Or in spiritual terms, the problem was not the heat but the heart.

A spiritually scorched life is due to a shortage of the water of life. However, the real issue is access to moisture rather than the absence of moisture. The difficulty is the barrier stone and not the brief shower. To enjoy healthy growth, plants and principles must be deeply rooted. Discoloration or disfigurement of a plant's surface is symptomatic of a much deeper problem. Similarly, when a person is not true to his colors ethically or spiritually, it suggests a spiritual rather than circumstantial cause.

Rocky Times

But the crucial question is, "Why am I rootless? Why am I disconnected from the people and priorities I profess to be important in my life? Why is my life unproductive and unfulfilling?" Jesus said the problem is the rock. The rock refers to hardened places of the heart that will not let the seed in all the way. It stands for mental rigidity in support of mistaken beliefs. The Word can go so far and no further. It can start its job but cannot finish. It can introduce joy but cannot sustain joy.

Like soil, the spirit has many layers, and the tendrils of truth must reach down to the deepest recesses of the soul. According to Jesus, the greatest priority of life is to love "with all the heart, with all the understanding, with all the soul, and with all the strength" (Mark 12:33). To love well, you must invite Christ's love deep into your heart. Paul's prayer in Ephesians 3:14-19 demonstrates this call to wholeheartedness and spiritual integrity:

> For this reason I bow my knees to the Father of our Lord Jesus Christ, from whom the whole family in heaven and earth is named, that He would grant you, according to the riches of His glory, to be strengthened with might through His Spirit in the inner man, that Christ may dwell in your hearts through faith; that you, being rooted and grounded in love, may be able to comprehend with all the saints what is the width and length and depth and height – to know the love of Christ which passes knowledge; that you may be filled with all the fullness of God.

To experience the fullness of God, your heart must overflow with the love of God (Romans 5:5). This is what it means to be "strengthened with might through His Spirit in the inner man." There can be no filling apart from knowing. When you are rooted and grounded in love, it is because Christ's Word dwells in you richly (Colossians 3:16). Therefore, fruitfulness cannot be separated from faith.

Yet something in people's hearts can prevent love from properly rooting. Jesus' image of a thick slab of stone impeding the growth of plants can represent any hindrance to believing and acting upon the information contained in the gospel. The rock stands for any wrongly held belief, attitude or habit that limits healthy human growth. Of all the obstructions to clear thinking and effective living, none is greater than fear.

Courageous Times

When people do not allow the Word of God to have its full affect in their lives, the limiting factor is usually fear. Jesus repeatedly reprimanded His disciples for allowing fear to get the best of their faith (Matthew 8:26). In its proper place, fear serves a beneficial purpose and can actually increase wisdom (Proverbs 1:7). But when fear is unreasonable, it undermines confidence in God's Word (Matthew 25:24-25; Revelation 21:8). Those who reject His counsel behave in ways that oppose their best interests.

Many kinds of debilitating fear exist. Some people are incapacitated by thoughts of failure; others are apprehensive about success. Some dread change while others grow uneasy when things stay the same. Some are terrified of becoming outcasts while others get nervous around crowds. Some have a morbid fear of death while others cannot stand the thought of another day. Whatever shape fear takes, it is a misguided form of self-protection. Facing fear is the key to desirable change. Three attributes help to loosen the iron grip of this scary adversary.

Faith

Faith in Jesus is a balm for anxious attitudes that shrink the soul. By trusting Christ you can correct the mistaken ideas that rob you of peace and stifle your spiritual growth. Courageous faith opens the door to new experiences that arise from fresh encounters with the living Word. It enables you to honor your conscience and keep your commitments. Moreover, it empowers you to serve the needy and protect the weak.

Hope

Hope is also needed to sustain courage. Hope anticipates the benefits of living in harmony with God's Word; fear anticipates the worst possible outcomes for daring to take God's promises seriously. It caused Aaron to cave to the crowd and mold a golden calf (Exodus 32). It led 10 spies to despair of defeating the armies of Canaan (Numbers 13:17–14:10). It led Peter to lurk in the shadows as Jesus was manhandled by enemies (John 18:15-27). Fear exaggerates the downside and minimizes the upside. It inflates the risks and ignores the rewards. It dampens initiative and discourages action. Hope puts fear in its place so you can retake your place on the path of progress.

Love

Most of all, love is the antidote to the heart-constricting effects of fear. Unloving thoughts are limiting thoughts. Like a farmer removing stones from a field, perfect love casts out fear. Disrespectful attitudes, hurtful words and abusive actions must go. Compassion displaces the narrow-minded rocks of prejudice and intolerance, and appropriate self-love dislodges destructive beliefs that underlie low self-esteem. To put it simply, the more you love, the better you grow.

Times of Refreshing

When faith, hope and love dry up, people are prone to give up. They stop growing and cease producing fruit for God's glory and the common good. They abandon their dreams and lose the desire for self-improvement. As a result, their souls begin to shrivel, and the withering continues until something changes in their hearts. Through repentance, the rocks that restrict growth are removed, and times of refreshing flow from the presence of the Lord (Acts 3:19).

The secret for harvesting spiritual fruit is putting down deep roots that supply your soul with living water. It is commitment born of conviction. But first you must discover what is holding you back and limiting your success. Find the rock! Remove the rock! And start enjoying the most fruitful season of your life.

Questions

1. What is the most important factor in successful living?

2. What is the ideal setting for a soul to flourish?

3. What was the problem with the second type of soil?

4. What happened to the plant that sprang up?

5. Why did the plant shrivel?

6. Why could the plant not find water?

7. When did the plant begin showing signs of distress?

8. What does the sun stand for in this story?

9. What does rocky soil figuratively represent?

10. Name three types of trials that test a person's faith.

Discussion Questions

1. Which trials are most notorious for causing Christians to fall away?

2. What is the significance of the rock being hidden?

3. How can people deepen the roots of their faith?

Assignment

Seed of the Week: Faithfulness

When and where can you sow a small seed of faithfulness this week? Nothing is more precious than the loyalty of people you love. What will you do to demonstrate your fidelity to a friend or family member?

Weed of the Week: Disloyalty

When someone has gone through a bad time, it is tempting to jump ship and abandon him. However, this is precisely when you should stand by his side. Never betray a friend's trust or give up on him. Do not excuse or enable bad behavior, but believe in him even when he cannot believe in himself.

Reflection and Prayer:

What do you reap when you sow more faithfulness and less fickleness on a daily basis? Ask God to help you be more dependable and less calculating this week.

CHAPTER 8

Thorny GROUND

How Free Is Your Heart?

"If you only care enough for a result, you will almost certainly attain it. Only you must then really wish these things, and wish them exclusively, and not wish at the same time a hundred other incompatible things just as strongly."
– Psychologist and philosopher William James

In the parable of the sower, Jesus was describing the unacceptable alternatives to a realistic and responsible life. Some people ignore life's greatest truths altogether. Others acknowledge their value but do not fully commit to them. In His third explanation of causes for a fruitless life, Jesus described the frustrating experience of the unfocused. Awareness of truth is a good thing, commitment to truth a better thing, but a laser-like focus on truth is the best thing.

Clarity, loyalty and integrity are the earmarks of a life well lived. The goal is to act upon truth to receive the benefits of living in harmony with the laws of life. Relationships are improved; the world is made better; God is pleased. What more could you want?

Yet people do not always respond favorably to God's Word or the helpful information that others would bring to their attention. Returning to Jesus' parable, note the progression in one's acquaintance with truth. With hard ground the seed does not get in at all. With rocky ground the seed gets in partially. With thorny ground the seed gets in all the way, but something interferes with its growth. When the seed (truth) does not fulfill its intended purpose, there is always a reason.

The Rise of the Rivals

In Jesus' third illustration, some seed fell on ground that was infested with pre-emergent weeds. The ground had been tilled and was receptive to the seed. It was free from rocks that could stop it from rooting deep in the earth. Yet something was desperately wrong. Unseen to the naked eye was a lethal army waiting to strike when the time was right. At first the farmer's seed sprang from the ground full of life and hope. But one day something distressing caught his eye. The farmer noticed a host of unwanted plants popping out of the ground to compete with his crop for the natural resources necessary for growth. As time passed, the weeds overtook his intended harvest. Jesus explained that the weeds represented three things that challenge the faith of His followers.

The Cares of This World

The most striking thing about this unholy trinity is that it does not contain anything inherently evil. Rather, the problem concerns mundane things that can dominate your life. Ordinary activities can consume all your time and attention if you let them (Matthew 6:25-34; Luke 10:38-42). Moreover, useless worry over things beyond your control can devour energy that might be put to better use (Matthew 6:27; Ephesians 5:15-16). To avoid becoming a slave to life's routines and uncertainties, scheduling your priorities is crucial. Otherwise, trifling things will kill your interest in vital things.

A neglected dream is like a forgotten present that was bought but never delivered. For safekeeping, you carefully stored it on a dark shelf in the back of your mind. And there it remains to this day. Until it is remembered and returned to the light, it will never warm a heart or draw a smile. As with gifts, so with goals: Out of sight, out of mind.

The Deceitfulness of Riches

Another thing that commonly competes for people's attention is money. When building wealth becomes all-consuming, disappointment is guaranteed. In Jesus' mind, the words "riches" and "deceitfulness" were a perfect fit. The word "deceitfulness" refers to something misleading in nature. It is not what it purports to be. Its boasts are hollow and false. No better description could be given to material wealth. Paul warned:

But those who desire to be rich fall into temptation and a snare, and into many foolish and harmful lusts which drown men in destruction and perdition. For the love of money is a root of all kinds of evil, for which some have strayed from the faith in their greediness, and pierced themselves through with many sorrows (1 Timothy 6:9-10).

Note the word "root." Materialism is not a static sin. It is a dynamic, growing thing with the vitality of kudzu. When loving money becomes more important than loving others, trouble is close behind. And when the desire to be rich outgrows the desire to be righteous, disaster looms. If left to itself, greed will overtake everything in your life. But for all the time and effort devoted to acquisition, the final payoff is little but sorrow. Worst of all, materialism is a self-inflicted wound in which you destroy your own heart while breaking the hearts of others. It is a sure but slow path to spiritual suicide.

Money exists to test our professed values (Matthew 19:16-30). More than a means of barter and exchange, it reveals the inner person in ways few things can. It does this by presenting us with choices. How we earn, save, spend and invest says a great deal about our values. Jesus asked, "What will a man give in exchange for his soul?" (16:26). Is honesty a commodity for sale? Is my pleasure more important than another's need (Luke 16:19-21)? Is achieving financial independence of greater value than extending mercy (12:13-21)?

In addition to testing your values, money is a means for training the soul. Every time you handle money, you are given an opportunity to become more Christlike. Ethical attainment builds honesty. Disciplined saving develops self-control. Generous giving promotes compassion. Financial transactions are spiritually transforming events. They are opportunities for practicing your faith, a kind of homework for the soul.

Those who see money as an end rather than a means have been sorely deceived. Satan would have us equate riches with security and happiness. No doubt, mishandling money can have unpleasant consequences, but amassing wealth is fraught with risks of its own. Although it is not a sin to become prosperous, affluence has never brought lasting happiness to a single soul. And in many cases, it has led to inconsolable heartache.

Peace and gladness are not wares to be bought in the world's market-place. They are byproducts of righteous living and loving relationships. They have more to do with practicing faith than padding portfolios.

To find more security in bank statements than God-statements is a clear sign of spiritual insolvency. The promises of God are the only sure things a person can bank on in life. Governments can be toppled and currency declared worthless. Markets can crash, and inflation can rise. Safes can be cracked, and computers can be hacked. Material wealth can evaporate into thin air in countless ways. Droughts, diseases and depressions are just a few of the ways one can go from riches to rags overnight. But one whose trust is in God and whose treasure is in heaven can never be poor or insecure (Psalm 23:1).

The Pleasures of Life

Luke's gospel adds one last worthless weed to complete the thorny troubles in Jesus' parable. Along with the cares of this world and the deceitfulness of riches, the pleasures of life can limit success by stifling the growth of God's children (Luke 8:14).

The word "pleasure" is not altogether negative. It refers to something that gives joy, delight or satisfaction. The origin of these emotions can be quite varied. On one hand, the source can be worldly, frivolous or sensual. An assortment of amusements falls into this first category. What they all have in common is shallowness. When these pleasurable feelings come and go, there is little to show for them.

A little recreation is a good thing, but leisure has a higher purpose than passing pleasure. Well-spent downtime should recharge your batteries and increase your productivity. A balanced life requires periods of renewal to restore energy and focus, but, ultimately, you must invest yourself in a worthy cause.

Sinful pleasure is repeatedly condemned in the Bible. Look at the following list and ask yourself, "What is the problem with the kind of pleasure in these verses?"

1. *1 Timothy 5:6:* "But she who **lives in pleasure** is dead while she lives."

    The key word in this verse is "lives." It describes a person who is constantly self-absorbed and stands in stark contrast with a godly life of good works (1 Timothy 5:3-10). When pleasing self becomes life's main purpose, people are spiritually dead although their bodies go on functioning for years. Do not live for the moment and the gratification of fleshly desires. Rather, live for eternal glory and the joy of serving others.

2. *2 Timothy 3:1-4:* "For know this, that in the last days perilous times will come: For men will be lovers of themselves, lovers of money, boasters, proud, blasphemers, disobedient to parents, unthankful, unholy, unloving, unforgiving, slanderers, without self-control, brutal, despisers of good, traitors, headstrong, haughty, **lovers of pleasure** rather than lovers of God."

   For a second time, Paul warns Timothy about the danger of living by the pleasure principle. The apostle identifies pleasure-seeking as the main motive behind a long list of crimes against humanity. Worst of all, it supplants love for God as the primary purpose of life. Great perils are in store for a society where people think more of themselves than their Maker.

3. *James 4:1-3:* "Where do wars and fights come from among you? Do they not come from your **desires for pleasure** that war in your members? You lust and do not have. You murder and covet and cannot obtain. You fight and war. Yet you do not have because you do not ask. You ask and do not receive, because you ask amiss, that you may **spend it on your pleasures**."

   When conflict is traced to its source, it generally has its roots in someone's obsession with pleasure. James referred to longings that underlie most disputes as "desires" or "lusts" rather than legitimate needs. Public discord reflects the private turmoil of a discontented soul. Sadly, longing of this kind can never be satisfied and is guaranteed to end in frustration.

4. *2 Thessalonians 2:11-12:* "And for this reason God will send them strong delusion, that they should believe the lie, that they all may be condemned who did not believe the truth but had **pleasure in unrighteousness**."

The problem here is not the seeking of pleasure but looking for it in the wrong places. Taking "pleasure in unrighteousness" refers to seeking satisfaction in ways that are fundamentally foolish and doomed to disappoint. This delusional thinking comes from rejecting what is true (biblical and ethical) and accepting what is false (mistaken and immoral).

In this brief review, pleasure has been clearly linked with condemnation, war, peril and death. Yet this is only half the story. Delight of a different kind will now be considered in the light of God's Word.

1. *Luke 12:32:* "Do not fear, little flock, for it is your **Father's good pleasure** to give you the kingdom."

2. *Philippians 2:12-13:* "Therefore, my beloved, as you have always obeyed, not as in my presence only, but now much more in my absence, work out your own salvation with fear and trembling; for it is God who works in you both to will and to do for **His good pleasure**."

3. *2 Thessalonians 1:11:* "Therefore we also pray always for you that our God would count you worthy of this calling, and fulfill all the **good pleasure of His goodness** and the work of faith with power."

In these verses the word most associated with God's pleasure is "good." This kind of pleasure is beneficial rather than destructive. God desires to give instead of take and to bless instead of burden. He wants the best for you and works tirelessly to that end. Pleasure of this kind is commendable and worthy of imitation.

Obviously, pleasure is not inherently evil. It all depends on the source of enjoyment or delight. Is it good or bad, righteous or unrighteous, selfish or unselfish? Even things that appear disagreeable on the surface actually may be desirable when viewed from a spiritual perspective. Paul said, "Therefore **I take pleasure** in infirmities, in reproaches, in needs, in persecutions, in distresses, for Christ's sake. For when I am weak, then I am strong" (2 Corinthians 12:10).

Legitimate forms of pleasure make a person better (stronger, holier and more Christlike). *Illegitimate* forms of pleasure keep people from achieving their full potential. They are exit ramps from the road of growth and improvement. They are distractions from your purpose and diversions from your priorities. Anything that (1) rivals love for God, (2) decreases concern for others, or (3) lessens respect for self is a worldly pleasure. It comes with a high price tag that includes plenty of regret and possible ruin. It is ambition without honor.

Mark called these yearnings "the desires for other things" (Mark 4:19). What "other" things? Things undeserving of your attention and affection. Things unhealthy and unholy. It is placing the sensual over the spiritual, the body before the soul, and the material above the relational. They are temporary, fleeting, hollow, disappointing things – things of the earth and not of eternity (Colossians 3:1-2); passing things and not permanent things (1 John 2:15-17). They are the things that compete for your love, challenge your loyalty, and contend for your very life. When the heart aches for what makes it break, it is hungering "for other things."

Suffocation of the Spirit

The principal danger of thorny ground is that the weeds will prevent the farmer's seed from bearing mature fruit. They do this by "choking" healthy plants as they struggle to grow, crowding and depriving them of the room and resources they need for development.

Jamming plants too closely together is a common problem with landscaping as well as gardening. Rather than spacing flowers, bushes and trees to accommodate their full growth potential, homeowners are tempted to disregard planting instructions and go for immediate visual impact. After a few seasons, the mistake becomes obvious as plants engulf one another.

Leyland cypress trees frequently suffer from this type of miscalculation. Because they are inexpensive and fast-growing, they are popular as a screen to hide neighboring houses. Seedlings are set close together to provide maximum privacy in minimal time. But after the branches touch in a few years, the growth has only begun. These towering giants rise 40 to 80 feet tall. As a result, they overwhelm each other along with fences, gutters, and anything else in their proximity. All living things need room to grow.

A different kind of problem occurs when people are corralled into close quarters. On May 23, 1883, President Chester Arthur and New

York Gov. Grover Cleveland dedicated the Brooklyn Bridge before more than 14,000 guests. A few days later a woman walking up the steps of the Manhattan side tripped, and her friend screamed. The shriek triggered a rumor that the bridge was about to collapse. In the panic that followed, 12 people were killed and 35 others were seriously injured. The deaths were due to suffocation, but the real cause was overcrowding. Sadly, this regrettable scene plays itself out time and time again at soccer stadiums and religious shrines across the world.

But congestion is not limited to highways or horticulture. Something very similar happens with ideas. The brain has a limited capacity to process information. When information overload occurs, some dreams and goals get lost in the shuffle. And even if they are retained in some measure, they will never come to fruition because they lack sufficient nurturing to reach maturity. It may be the dream of a new life in Christ or a personal goal that uniquely expresses your personality, but something valuable is lost when the mind exceeds its capacity to pay attention.

Ideas, like plants, must be encouraged. If neglected, they will languish. If supported, they will flourish. Concentration is to goals what weeding and spacing is to gardens: The fewer the distractions, the greater the fruit. Or to put it more simply, less is more.

Barrenness of the Soul

In Jesus' parable, the goal of the sower was to reap a bountiful harvest when the day of gathering arrived. On another occasion, Christ used the image of a vineyard to emphasize the prolific growth of which humans are capable and for which God will hold them responsible (John 15:1-11). Whether grain or grapes, the lesson is clear: A fruitful life is not merely optional or desirable; it is expected and demanded!

The grain that grew amidst thorns and weeds did not die; it simply did not bring fruit to maturity. Bible students debate the meaning of the fruit metaphor. Does it refer to harvesting souls for the Savior or to cultivating the fruit of the Spirit? Surely, it is both. The goal of the Christian life is to please and honor God by doing something useful for others during our lifetimes on earth. Fruit satisfies human needs and sparks human growth. We must be fruit and bear fruit for our heavenly Father. We must be useful.

Like plants, no two people are endowed with the same capacity for growth (Matthew 25:14-30). The key is not to compare and compete. The challenge is to become the best person you can be for the glory of God. Settling for a mediocre life dishonors your God and your potential. Discover your gifts and use them to their fullest. Define your dreams, and give them your all. The soul suffers when dreams are neglected and talents are buried. Therefore, the Master Gardener implores, "Do not sow among thorns" (Jeremiah 4:3). When you finally get focused, the fruit will come.

Questions

1. What did the seed fall among in Jesus' third analogy?

2. What happened to the plants that sprang from the sower's seed?

3. Name three things that choke the Word of God.

4. What did the thorns keep the fruit from doing?

5. What kinds of cares choke the Word (Matthew 13:22)?

6. What is the danger of riches (Matthew 13:22)?

7. Name two things money can do to a person.

8. What word is most associated with God's pleasure?

9. In what did Paul take pleasure (2 Corinthians 12:10)?

10. What do legitimate forms of pleasure do for a person?

Discussion Questions

1. What are the thorns that compete for your attention?

2. How is the love of money like a root?

3. How can Christians stay focused on what really matters?

Assignment

Seed of the Week: Gentleness

When and where will you sow a small seed of gentleness this week? To treat others gently will require two things: humility and empathy. A person who is modest and mindful will enjoy better relationships than one who is conceited and inconsiderate.

Weed of the Week: Harshness

When you treat people roughly and rudely, it is because of pride. You are thinking too much about yourself and too little about them. Make up your mind that you will never treat another person cruelly or callously.

Reflection and Prayer:

What do you reap when you sow more gentleness and less harshness on a daily basis? Ask God to help you become meeker and less abrasive this week.

CHAPTER 9

Good
GROUND
The Soil of Success

"Seeds, like hearts, must open to grow."
– Author Carol Horos

Throughout the centuries and across the continents, people from every culture have shared one thing in common: they were searching for the secret to a more successful life. But where will such a monumental discovery be found? Will it come from the arena of politics, finance, health care or conservation?

The common thread is that people in every field of endeavor (educators, entrepreneurs, entertainers, ecologists, economists, engineers, etc.) are trying to make the world better by implementing new ideas that will solve problems, alleviate suffering and increase joy. The same thing takes place when families gather around kitchen tables and individuals reflect in coffee shops or quiet parks. Through contemplation, dialogue and action, the world is made better one thought at a time. More and better thinking are precursors to success.

In the parable of the sower, Jesus offered a comprehensive solution to mankind's yearning for peace, progress and prosperity. The answer does not lie in the technical discoveries of any single discipline. Instead, the key is for every individual to master the universal principles of success found in spiritual living. By elevating thinking in general, a foundation is laid for fruitful living. By becoming a better person overall, qualities of goodness are brought to bear on all of one's activities. This is what good soil is about: establishing the most fertile ground possible for growth, achievement and fulfillment. Success begins with cultivating the depth of character necessary for abundant living. It requires a refined disposition and rigorous discipline.

People are four-dimensional beings composed of body, mind, heart and soul. As a result, humans have four kinds of primary needs: physical, mental, emotional and spiritual. Therefore, the ultimate answer to what ails mankind must be as balanced as human nature and as broad as humankind. Any solution that does not address all people and all that is in people is insufficient to satisfy the needs and longings of the soul. It must work for men and women; rich and poor; rural and urban; minorities and majorities; self-learners and college graduates. Bottom line: Whenever it is applied, it should work.

Four Unbreakable Laws

In the opening section of this book, we uncovered the four laws of success embedded in Jesus' parable. The first and most basic was the *law of the seed* that says all things bring forth after their kind. This law of cause and effect is no respecter of persons and meets the standard of universal application. It applies to all people at all times in all places. You get in life what you sow.

Next came the *law of the sower,* which maintains that all people are endowed with free will to choose the seeds (thoughts, words and deeds) they will sow. The key to a successful life is to choose seeds that correspond with the harvest you want to reap. Choices may be temporarily and circumstantially limited by factors beyond your control. However, you are never without viable options for achieving your major purpose of becoming your best self to the glory of God. If you are not getting what you want and need in life, the answer is to make better choices.

The *law of the soil* says that growth and genuine success are rooted in your receptivity to truth. When truth is rejected or its influence limited, it cannot produce the benefits it was intended to provide. Truth must be given free course to bring its fruit to maturity. Denial, delusion and distraction keep people from engaging life realistically and responsibly.

Personal growth and meaningful achievement require increasing amounts of honesty and accountability.

The final maxim was the *law of the sickle*. This unbreakable law holds that the harvest you are currently reaping is the result of seeds you have sown in the past. Therefore, the life you hope for tomorrow will be determined by the seeds you sow today. Success is more about wise sowing than wishful thinking and more about diligence than daydreaming. With this law in hand, you can create a better tomorrow by deliberately and consistently sowing the future you most desire. Success is about living a more purposeful life by harnessing the power of intention.

Four Possible Soils

Understanding the power of choice in shaping your life is just the beginning. Knowing what you want and believing in yourself as an agent of constructive change must be linked with an attitude that supports growth. In the last three chapters, we saw how people can sabotage their success by laying the groundwork for failure. Now it is time to look at the positive side of the equation: the good ground of a fruitful life.

This dream soil is the antithesis of the deficient soils previously discussed. Good soil describes the ideal context for unleashing the power contained in the seed of truth and the soul of man. It represents a human being's optimal learning, working and growing mindset. Many ways of thinking are unproductive. Jesus now addresses the most favorable frame of mind for a fruitful and fulfilling life. In doing so, His desire is that hearers will conduct an honest study of their hearts with a readiness to change whatever is holding them back from becoming the best person they can be.

How Broken Is Your Spirit?

If hard ground depicts a person who is unmindful as he journeys through life, then good ground must stand for a person with a tender, teachable heart (James 1:21). Openness to truth and counsel is fundamental to success. It is also the ground of healthy self-esteem (Proverbs 11:14). A strong person considers the viewpoints of those who see things differently. That is why pride is a sign of weakness and a herald of future sadness. Conversely, humility is a sign of strength and a harbinger of future greatness. You must be able to acknowledge fallibility to enter the narrow gate and travel the difficult path of personal transformation. Change for the better is not possible until you can look your limitations square in the eye (2 Corinthians 12:7-10). The lesson of the hard ground is the value of humility and self-honesty.

It is impossible to correct shortcomings and compensate for blind spots without a broken spirit (Psalm 51:17). Neither is it feasible to maintain good relationships without meekness. Arrogance and insensitivity are precursors to loneliness (Matthew 7:1-5). Few people enjoy the company of someone who is conceited or critical, but most people enjoy being around someone who is caring and kind. A meek person inherits the earth (5:5); a smug person alienates the earth.

Like soft, receptive soil, a sensitive soul is the fertile ground of personal growth. It takes keen self-awareness to become a bigger person. It takes an expanding awareness of others to create a better world. When hearts harden, they become less thoughtful and less kind. Selfishness and callousness are the leading causes of unhappiness in the world.

How Deep Is Your Love?

If rocky ground represents a shallow person whose level of commitment is limited, then good ground must represent a person of unyielding dedication. Full, unbending devotion is a rare thing, and few are willing to pay such a high price for their vision and values. But spiritual stamina is essential to enjoy a life of effectiveness. The lesson of the rocky ground is the necessity of commitment for growth and success.

While hard-ground people evade serious thought, rocky-ground people fail to think things all the way through. They see benefits but not costs. They see results but ignore process. Consequently, they seldom finish what they start. When the going gets tough, they move on to something less demanding. They give up precisely when it is time to dig in.

Most projects – including self-improvement – share three things:

1. They are harder than you think.

2. They take longer than you think.

3. They cost more than you think.

That is why positive change is unlikely to occur without true dedication. Breaking with self-destructive habits takes faith and fortitude; making a marriage work takes strength and steadfastness; completing important goals takes resolve and resilience. Depth of commitment comes from depth of character. Those who are frivolous and flighty lack the courage and discipline it takes to be successful. They wilt under life's weight. They start but do not stick.

Successful people have staying power. They have cultivated the ability to do things that less successful people are unwilling to do. They are motivated more by long-term payoffs than by short-term pleasures. When they make a promise, it is not up for negotiation. They do not ask if keeping their word and maintaining their honor is convenient. Their philosophy is, "Do the right thing, the right way, at the right time, whether you feel like it or not." Tenacity is the trademark of the triumphant.

How Free Is Your Heart?

The lesson of the thorny ground is the power of purpose. If thorny ground describes a person who lacks focus, then good ground must represent a person in touch with his values, goals and priorities. Maintaining this kind of focus is not easy. To do so requires two special competencies: developing mindfulness and overcoming forgetfulness. Some kinds of forgetting can be useful (forgiveness for example), but losing sight of your purpose is never helpful (Philippians 3:13-14).

Cultivating Mindfulness

To reinforce mindfulness, it is important to clarify your goals. Write them down. Describe them in graphic detail. Meditate on them. Share them with others. Post them in prominent places. Begin a dream journal. Construct a vision board. Identify milestones. Set target dates. Specify next steps. Designate rewards. Get an accountability partner. Choose a mentor. Hire a coach. Join a support group.

These tactics will help you to take consistent, fervent, abundant action. Sowing frequently and lavishly are vital to success, but without mindfulness it will not happen. Depending on whim or willpower to get things done is unrealistic. Set yourself up for success by understanding the way your mind works and using it to your advantage. Do not wait for your moods to move you or for the stars to align in your favor. Your future rests in your hands. Take action today, and support it with tools and strategies that reinforce mindfulness.

Curbing Forgetfulness
The second skill successful people have developed is the ability to recognize and minimize things that distract them from their goals. Here are 10 ways your attention can be diverted from what matters most:

• *Over-promising:* Learn to say no and mean it. Get rid of guilt by reminding yourself about the commitments you would have compromised by taking on too much. Every "no" is a "yes" to a greater value, and every "yes" is a "no" to a lesser value.

• *Over-scheduling:* Quit kidding yourself about time commitments. Be honest about commute, preparation and recovery time. Leave yourself breathing room for handling the unexpected. The less stressed you are, the more you are on top of your game. Keep your cool, and you will keep your focus.

• *Over-connecting:* In our high-tech world, it is possible to be too available. Digital distractions (e-mail, texting and calls) can easily disrupt concentration and work flow. To maintain your pace and productivity, limit social media to appropriate times, and do not yield to everyone's demand for your immediate attention. Remember, technology is your servant, not your master.

• *Blaming:* Anything that takes your attention off solving the problem at hand is detrimental. Blaming requires looking backward; success requires looking forward. And before blasting someone, be sure to consider your own part in the problem. Ask yourself what you might do differently next time to get a more desirable result. Can I communicate better? Can I provide more direction or encouragement? Concentrating on solutions produces better results than blaming.

• *Complaining:* Complaining is the least constructive thing a person can do when problems arise because it consumes massive amounts of energy without adding anything of value. It is a bad habit with as much social appeal as chewing your fingernails. Even worse, it is contagious and can contaminate your whole environment. Make your life a complaint-free zone, and use your energy for something more constructive (Philippians 2:14).

• *Explaining:* Explaining is different from complaining and blaming because it attributes failure to extenuating circumstances. Although less offensive, the negative effect is the same: Explainers fail to take ownership of their choices by disavowing responsibility. It is a sophisticated form of learned helplessness. As Ben Franklin once said, "I never knew a person who was good at making excuses who was good at anything else." The danger with excuses is that we often believe them. Explanations are really just excuses in disguise. Do not blame, complain or explain; just change!

• *Exceptions:* Exceptions are the giant of commitment killers. Selectively disengaging from your goals and values is the first step along the road that leads away from the life you want. "Just this once" is a mental game we play to reduce our guilt feelings. It lets us convince ourselves that the price for behaving contrary to our desires will be negligible. It is a lie extraordinaire. When it comes to core commitments, enforce the no-exception rule.

• *Critics:* Negative people are well-meaning but highly destructive. They are experts at identifying problems and highlighting shortcomings but incapable of seeing blessings, strengths and possibilities. As a result, their viewpoints are skewed and overly pessimistic. As much as possible, limit your time with toxic people who constantly sow seeds of doubt and discouragement in your life.

• *Ingratitude:* It is impossible to enjoy fullness of life without a thankful life. The first sin was provoked by discontent, and the last sin will be no different (not to mention every sin in between). A grateful heart is productive. An ungrateful heart is destructive. Be thankful, and you will be more fruitful.

• *Negativity:* Pessimistic thinking comes from internalizing the negativity of those around us (parents, friends, co-workers, etc.). Over time we play the same depressing tapes in our heads until they are confused with reality. Patterns of gloomy thinking keep us from success by clouding vision. A negative person is like a nervous driver caught in a thick fog. He cannot see his potential or life's possibilities, but he is skilled at imagining carnage around every corner. Without throwing caution to the wind, choose to live your life confidently and expectantly. By putting your hopes ahead of your fears, you will find more happiness and success throughout your lifetime.

Paul wrote that "Christ has made us free" (Galatians 5:1). Free hearts are fruitful hearts, but what does liberty in Christ mean? Above all, it is deliverance from the constricting forces of life. It is letting go of the person you are, to become the person you were created to be (Luke 17:33). It is a combination of salvation and sanctification. It is unleashing potential by unshackling the heart.

How Is Your Harvest?

Everything you become and achieve in your lifetime will come from your heart. Character and accomplishments are the natural outgrowth of your spirit's deepest longings. When your intellect, emotions and will work in unison, the likelihood of a fruitful life is increased.

The most impressive part of the parable of the sower is the amazing yield produced by the good ground. Similarly, when the heart is good, the results are simply astounding. This is the place where you experience a tipping point in productivity and growth. Effectiveness and satisfaction increase exponentially with integrity. But rewards and respect are not for careless souls who wander aimlessly through life. Commendation is reserved for those who contribute to the world's betterment through faith in Christ and His teaching.

The bottom line is that good soil bears fruit. But what constitutes good soil? Jesus said that good hearts can be identified by three responses to God's Word:

- They understand it (Matthew 13:23); *"I get it!"*
- They accept it (Mark 4:20); *"I love it!"*
- They keep it (Luke 8:15); *"I'll do it!"*

Comprehending, embracing and obeying the Bible's message are sequential steps in the process of spiritual growth. *Comprehending* God's Word has more to do with diligence than intelligence. *Embracing* God's Word has more to do with love than logic. And *obeying* God's Word has more to do with gratitude than gray matter. Christianity is not unintelligent, illogical or unreasonable, but nobility of heart is what enables people to use their higher powers effectively. Or as Jesus put it, only those who hunger and thirst after righteousness can be filled. A longing for truth is the most important factor in living a fruitful life (Matthew 5:6). Therefore, wisdom has less to do with your IQ (intelligence quotient) than DQ (desire quotient).

He Who Has Ears

Before concluding His message, Jesus offered His audience one last word of advice: "He who has ears to hear, let him hear!" (Matthew 13:9). Jesus was reminding his listeners that the conditions of their lives were largely of their own making. He knew many would not be receptive to that truth, but that a few would take His counsel to heart. They would meditate on His words and not let them drift from their consciousness. They would commit wholeheartedly to following His teaching regardless of the costs. They would refuse to let lesser things interfere with life's supreme commitments. These principles are the key to achieving a breakthrough in better living because they reveal what it takes to change for good.

Those who relinquish control of their lives to external factors will never know genuine success. Those who rise above circumstances by exercising greater control over their thoughts will never know true failure. The difference lies in the source of control. One person is manipulated by what others think, say or do. The other is motivated by his own purpose, values and goals. One is reactive and passively accepts whatever life hands him. The other is proactive and assertively challenges the status quo. Healthy thinking sparks prudent action that leads to positive results. But never forget, it all begins with a good heart.

Hazy plans and half-hearted efforts are not the stuff of success. Life demands more from those to whom it gives its most precious fruits. And God demands more from those who would know His richest blessings. Singleness of mind, purity of heart and constancy of purpose are the benchmarks of spiritual success.

Section Review

- "Hard ground" means lack of awareness (no change).

- "Rocky ground" means lack of commitment (temporary change).
- "Thorny ground" means lack of focus (trivial change).
- "Good ground" means awareness, commitment and focus (thorough change).

Questions

1. What was the fourth type of ground in this parable?

2. What did this soil yield?

3. What kind of heart does good ground represent?

4. What do these people do with God's Word?

5. What happens when they obey God's Word?

6. What virtue is necessary to bear fruit?

7. What is the precursor to success?

8. What does this author say good soil represents?

9. What does "liberty in Christ" mean?

10. What challenge did Jesus issue at the close of the parable?

Discussion Questions

1. Why does everything you become and achieve depend on your heart?

2. What does this parable reveal about the way change occurs?

3. Why is DQ more important than IQ?

Assignment

Seed of the Week: Self-control

When and where will you sow a small seed of self-control this week? Success is measured by the power you exercise over your thoughts, words and deeds. The more disciplined you are, the happier and more effective you will be.

Weed of the Week: Self-indulgence

When you give in to your lusts or bad moods, harmful things happen. Every surrender becomes a stain on your character and reputation. Respect and honor come from doing the right thing, not the easy thing.

Reflection and Prayer:

What do you reap when you sow more self-control and less self-indulgence on a daily basis? Ask God to help you be more in-control and less out-of-control this week.

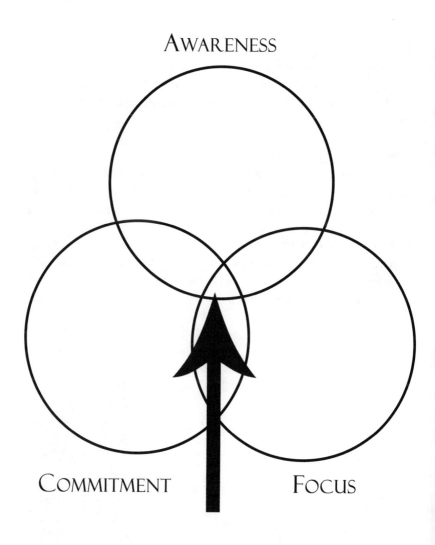

Good soil exists precisely at the intersection
of awareness, commitment and focus.

The SEEDS

The problem with seeds is size. They are tiny, yet full of amazing energy. Because they are petite, many people underestimate their potency. Christians ought never to make that mistake. Those familiar with the sower story delight in the small. They know that little is not always less. They realize the value of small words of encouragement, little acts of kindness, and tiny seeds of faith.

In Section Three of this book, you will be challenged to put the power of the Seed Principle to work in your life. It is a no-nonsense, results-oriented approach to living. By sowing purposefully, plentifully and persistently, your seed-size efforts will produce astounding results.

One of the best things about the Seed Principle is that it works in every sphere of life. In Chapter 10 you will learn how it can help you to manage your spiritual growth to increase your joy, confidence and influence. In Chapter 11 you will see how it can be used to turn troubled relationships into caring connections. And in Chapter 12 you will discover how to use the Seed Principle to turn a struggling church, business or volunteer organization into a thriving team.

In the final chapter of this book, you will be introduced to a powerful tool to help you reap a more rewarding life. It is called "The Sower's

Almanac" because it allows you to forecast success. By asking the right questions and sowing the right seeds, you can produce positive results with surprising consistency. The future always holds uncertainties, but those who understand the secrets of the sower exercise more control over their lives than those who do not.

Success is not a mystery. It is mastery of four simple gardening principles. Put them into practice and begin sowing the life of your dreams:

- Know what you want to harvest.
- Sow corresponding seed.
- Create a growth environment.
- Persevere to the end.

"He who sows bountifully will also reap bountifully."
(2 Corinthians 9:6)

CHAPTER 10

Sowing Seeds of
SPIRITUAL GROWTH
Improving Myself, One Seed at a Time

*"All the flowers of all the tomorrows are
in the seeds of today."*
– Unknown

Humans develop in different ways (Luke 2:52), but the most mean-ingful kind of growth is spiritual. Enlarging your soul increases the capacity for every useful endeavor. It is growth of competency in life.

Spirituality is concerned with life's greatest realities. Much more to life exists than the material world perceived by the five senses. The spiritual world may be invisible, but it is more real – or at least more enduring – than the physical world.

- People or beings that you cannot presently see include:

    Angels and demons

    Deceased but living persons

    God the Father, Son and Spirit

- Places or realms that you cannot immediately view include:

    The blessedness of paradise

    The awfulness of hell

    The glory of heaven

- And things or entities that you cannot directly observe include:

The eternal soul

The stain of sin

The presence of love

God in His wisdom placed these otherworldly things just beyond the horizon of sensory experience and scientific investigation. But what cannot be grasped with "standard" equipment can be known through the faculty of faith. Spiritual truth is not beyond man's grasp, but a humbler path is required to receive it.

Faith is a precious gift available to all but appreciated by few. By faith, human beings come in contact with transcendent reality. Faith is not a flight into fantasy. Faith is the "substance" of things hoped for and the "evidence" of things not seen (Hebrews 11:1). It is the means God provided for understanding life's deepest values, and the tool God gave for shaping a more desirable future. Faith is not cowardly withdrawal but courageous advancement. Faith is God's instrument for interacting with all that lies beyond the moment and the material.

To grow spiritually is to heighten your connection to the spiritual world without withdrawing from the physical world. Christians are to set their affection on things above while leading full lives on the earth below. They love and serve earthly beings without undue attachment to earthly belongings. Their spirituality brings greater presence and perspective to everyday existence.

Spiritual people do not devalue their bodies, but neither do they overplay the importance of the flesh. The body possesses dignity but not divinity. It is to be honored but not worshiped. It is servant and not master. Therefore, a prudent person distinguishes between the body's needs and its desires.

Christians are positively pro-body but always give priority to the higher, nobler, indestructible spirit of man. The human body is tool, vessel or container. The human spirit is its life, energy and force. The body exerts a powerful influence upon the spirit, but the spirit was always intended to prevail. When the roles are reversed, bad things happen. Therefore, attention should be directed continually to awakening, enlarging and sanctifying the spirit.

Sowing Spiritual Thoughts

A person who seeks to grow spiritually commits himself to a special kind of inward growth. Eastern faiths and New Age mysticism encourage a kind of religious experience that bypasses the mind. Christians are committed to elevating the mind rather than circumventing it. No one can grow closer to God by shutting off thought. Rather, by activating the mind, beneficial change occurs. When the psalmist declared, "Be still, and know that I am God" (Psalm 46:10), he was not praising mental laziness or inactivity as a path to God. Rather, he was encouraging worshipers to slow the pace of life so that more thinking could be devoted to understanding God and His Word.

Spiritual people engage in right thinking, but right thinking is more than accumulating bundles of facts. It is learning how to reason in a godly way (1 Corinthians 1:10). The Bible corrects faulty thinking and establishes clear boundaries between right and wrong. However, possessing the mind of Christ is more than mastering lists of appropriate and inappropriate behavior. It is learning to live more mindfully. Spiritually minded people operate on a higher plane of consciousness and are more self-aware than the average person. They are more thoughtful about their actions and more considerate of the needs of others.

Still, spiritual growth is more than deep thinking (1 Corinthians 2:14-16). It is linking the mind with its Maker through sacred Scripture. Human reason without the aid of inspired revelation has severe limitations. What is knowable through the senses is prone to distortion due to man's self-interest (1:20-21). Spiritual growth requires thinking that is holy and holistic. It is the result of thinking alertly, ethically and biblically at the same time.

Man's spiritual faculties are not limited to logic alone. Feelings are emotionally charged thoughts that emerge spontaneously from the subconscious. Passion and intuition draw on hidden stores of knowledge derived from a lifetime of experience. Unsolicited promptings of this kind are memos from the past embedded in the neural pathways of the body. They are the sticky notes of the soul, the communication system of the conscience. Those who ignore these powerful messages do so at their own peril.

These cues alert you to dangers and opportunities you might otherwise overlook. They cut through the normal deliberation process to encourage or dissuade a course of action. Although they contain wisdom and motivational power, they also can be difficult to read. The key is to proceed cautiously. There is something valuable to be investigated, but the meaning can be encrypted and requires careful deciphering. What they share is a common plea for you to pay closer attention.

To be strong in the Lord and the power of His might is to develop a mental toughness of the spiritual kind. It is strength of thought fortified by faith, hope and love. It is God-centered, heaven-leading, people-focused thought. Thinking clearly and compassionately is the foundation of living well, and this discipline is developed one thought at a time. Therefore, spiritual growth begins when elevated ideas are fixed in the mind and absorbed in the soul (Psalm 119:11). Only then can truth set you free from the painful consequences of ignorance and sinfulness (John 8:32).

Sowing Spiritual Habits

Because developing the mind of Christ is the key to spiritual growth, it is useful to develop the habits of Christ. No habit is more essential to successful growth than a powerful prayer life. Start by sowing simple mealtime prayers expressing gratitude for your blessings. Meal prayers are proper in view of God's goodness, but they also create momentum for thinking in a more spiritual way throughout the day. The mind is centered on God rather than self and on blessings rather than problems. It may seem like a small step, but it is definitely a move in the right direction.

A person who has mastered the practice of mealtime prayer will want to progress to deeper, more extended times of communion with God. Sowing the seed of a morning prayer sets the tone for all of a Christian's waking hours. Sowing an afternoon prayer strengthens the spirit by refocusing attention on spiritual priorities. Sowing an evening prayer settles the mind for peaceful rest that is crucial for the next day's activities.

Prayer Is Like Exercise

As you develop your spiritual growth plan, make morning prayer a top priority because it will help you start each day on the right track. Other occasions of prayer will follow naturally. It will take willpower to get started, but do not wait until you feel more spiritual to begin. The better feelings you seek will be a byproduct of having prayed. Prayer is a lot like running. Few beginners enjoy crawling out of bed, getting dressed, and putting in that first mile. However, everyone loves having run once they are finished. Keep your eye on the goal, and the good feelings you seek will follow as you increase your consistency. During these fuller prayer times, make it your goal to be unhurried. Do not get hung up on the quantity of time spent in prayer. Instead, go for quality by being wholly present and absolutely authentic. Rushing through stock prayers does not impress Christ or improve character. Hasty, perfunctory prayers only serve to fool the petitioner about his spiritual condition. Patient, thoughtful prayers are the stuff of growth. The critical factor is not the duration of the prayer but the relationship between the petitioner and God. Enjoying God's presence gives prayer a delight and vibrancy that stretch the soul to new dimensions.

How to Prioritize Prayer

Knowing the value of prayer and how to pray does not guarantee that you will actually spend time praying. The practice of prayer takes real effort, especially in the beginning. The first thing to do is prioritize prayer. Although life is filled with pressing duties, you can actually get more done by pausing to get spiritually centered before launching into activity. The more you have to do, the more important it is to connect with your spiritual power source.

Prayer brings clarity and energy to daily tasks. It transforms ordinary work into sacred business. It changes drudgery into delight and to-do lists into labors of love. Prayer puts a new frame on old routines by bringing perspective and passion to the day's affairs.

Prioritizing prayer means rendering it non-negotiable. In the course of any day, a person enjoys many things he can do without if necessary: 10 extra minutes of sleep, the morning news, a dash to the coffee shop during the commute to work. But when push comes to shove, prayer must not be set aside. It is like dressing. No matter how big a hurry you are in, you do not fail to clothe yourself.

Imagine explaining to your boss, "I was running late, so I decided not to wear shoes and socks today." If the boss did not fire you for lack of judgment, she would immediately send you home to get properly attired. You simply are not ready for business until this is done.

Similarly, no one is ready for managing life's relationships and responsibilities until he has clothed his mind in prayer. He is spiritually naked and has left his armor hanging in the closet. If you do not have time to pray, get back in bed, pull up the covers, and try again tomorrow. But better yet, realize that you do have time to bow your head and meet with your Maker about the business of the day.

Invest to Be Your Best

Other disciplines that provide a foundation for spiritual growth include worship and study of God's Word. Each worship assembly and Bible class becomes a vital part of the fabric of your personal faith. They are investments in the person you want to become. Human development comes from dominant thoughts that focus the mind and challenge the soul. Thoughts about God's power and goodness lead to a confident and kind life. Thoughts about Jesus' mercy and love lead to a gracious and compassionate life. A few minutes in God's Word and presence can make all the difference in the outcome of a day. To end well, you must begin well.

Neglecting the soul's need for worship and study is more costly than most people realize. Mysterious problems begin to surface that seem unrelated to religious matters. Deeper reflection reveals that disengaging from the church has complicated your relationships and compromised your goals. Ever so slightly, you are out of sync. The truth is that where no seed is sown, no fruit can be grown. So, what is the answer? Plant the seed! The key to a better future is not wishful thinking but careful sowing of spiritual seeds in increasing abundance.

Sowing Spiritual Attitudes

The Seed Principle is especially helpful for improving attitudes. For example, by sowing seeds of gratitude, you become happier and more hopeful about life. Ingratitude, on the other hand, robs you of joy and initiative. In either case, the choice is yours. Circumstances do not produce your attitude. You bring your attitude to your circumstances.

Most of what you experience in life is the result of seeds you have sown or failed to sow in the past. Understanding this fact is one of the most liberating moments you will ever know. God uses experience to show you the choices you have made. Your job is to pay attention and learn. But even when sorrow and suffering stem from conditions beyond your control, you still must choose how to respond to undesirable experiences. When you cannot choose your circumstances directly, you can still choose your attitude, and before long your attitude can help bring about a new and better set of circumstances. Paul could rejoice in a Roman prison, and Jesus could forgive his persecutors while hanging on a Roman cross. The same principle works in the present century no less than in the first century.

Life Is How You Look at It
My friend Alan has been a police officer in Atlanta for 18 years. When off duty he operates his own home improvement business. While he was doing a project for me, we struck up a conversation and he shared a little of his life story.

Alan was adopted as an infant and raised by a caring couple who showered him with love. One day after he was grown and had a wife and son of his own, his mother asked him if he would like to meet his biological mother. Alan's first impulse was to decline. His upbringing was filled with wonderful memories, and he felt no emotional hole demanding to be filled. But after some reflection, he decided there were good reasons why such a meeting might be beneficial.

A couple of weeks later, Alan got a call from his mom saying his birth mother had been located and that she had agreed to meet face-to-face with him. Arrangements were made, and the day of reunion finally arrived. Tension filled the air, but it was the good kind of feeling one gets when looking forward to one of life's rare and precious moments. It turned out to be a day of joy and more than a few surprises.

Alan asked his birth mother if she knew his biological father; she replied, "Yes, and I married him. He is seated beside me right now." She had been a young teacher at a religious school when Alan was conceived out of wedlock. Thinking she would be fired and shunned, she decided it was best for her son to grow up in a more stable home. As it turned out, she had made a wise choice.

But another question was pressing on Alan's mind. For many years he had wondered if he had any siblings. Before answering, his birth mother told him, "You might want to sit down." Then came the astonishing news: "You have three brothers." It took a little time to break the story to relatives and friends, but since that day, several happy gatherings have taken place. Alan's family had more than doubled overnight.

Imagine waking up one day and discovering you have three younger brothers, two sisters-in-law, and a niece and nephew you never knew existed. After 30 years of separation, how would you choose to respond? No doubt some would bristle and bemoan the injustice of time lost – but not Alan. He did not ask to be adopted, but he rejoiced that two loving people chose to call him by their name and make room for him in their hearts. How could there be regrets when he had been loved so much and cared for so well? How could there be bitterness when life's circumstances led him to the girl of his dreams and the son he adores? The way Alan looks at life, he simply uncovered a whole new set of blessings for which to be grateful. You see, life is how you look at it, and in most cases, the short end of the stick is more about shortsightedness than the length of the stick.

Sowing Spiritual Virtues

Whatever qualities you want to develop to make your life more honorable and useful, the process for acquiring them is essentially the same. The following four steps summarize the stages you must go through to realize your potential and make your dream life a reality.

(1) Reflection: The process of personal change takes a giant step forward when you get a clear picture of the person you want to become. This shift of identity is the most compelling force that drives change. It provides both a goal to aspire to and motivation to pursue it. Guilt and shame make you aware of the need for change, but it takes a more positive force to endure over the long haul. The more you think and talk about what you desire, the more likely you are to experience it. So, if you are not growing as fast as you would like, what meditations might move things along?

(2) Responsibility: Once a person forms a powerful new self-image, he must take full responsibility for making the necessary changes to realize his dream. Spiritual growth does not occur by magic. It takes serious study and lots of sacrifice. Others may help along the way, but personal growth is not possible apart from tough choices and self-discipline. There is no easy alternative. Personal responsibility is the exacting path that leads to the better life you desire. Stand in front of the mirror, look yourself square in the eye, and repeat these words: "My life will change only when I do."

(3) Resolve: When a clear vision of a better life has been formulated, and when you accept the stubborn fact that you are primarily responsible for improving your situation, the time has come for committed action. Resolve is the gritty combination of initiative and stick-to-itiveness. It is tenacity and doggedness in following your heart's desires. It is adopting a "whatever it takes" mindset and paying the price to achieve your dreams.

Growth requires action and not just contemplation. Make it a habit to practice whatever you want more of in your life. Do not center all your attention on the negative quality you hope to overcome. Instead, dwell on the positive attributes you want to develop. That is where your most profitable work will be done.

- *Gossiping.* To overcome gossip, practice saying something positive about those whom you meet and discuss. It might just become a habit!

- *Judging.* To overcome being judgmental, practice listening to others patiently without interrupting. When they are finished talking, ask them if they have anything they would like to add before you comment.

- *Arguing.* To overcome arguing, practice speaking slowly and softly and staying focused on solutions rather than defending yourself.

- *Anger.* To overcome anger, practice believing the very best about others' intentions (isn't that what you would want?). Also, ask yourself how you may have contributed to the problem. What could you do next time to get a better result?

- *Depression.* To overcome discouragement, select one thing you think will improve your situation, and do it promptly. Discouragement is a clue that different actions are in order.

(4) Resilience: Jesus told His followers they should be ready to forgive others at least 490 times ("70 times seven"; Matthew 18:22). The point is that the change process is challenging, and there will be many slip-ups along the way. Do not be discouraged by setbacks. They are a normal part of growth. Make contingency plans instead of surrender plans. And do not forget to surround yourself with encouraging relationships to support your efforts. Successful living is done with the help of a caring community rather than in isolation (Galatians 6:2). Admitting you are not superhuman and asking for help is a sign of spiritual progress. In the end, the key to growth is not giving up. Every lapse is a learning opportunity to be mined for insights that will put you one step closer to success next time.

Take Control by the Seeds You Sow

Spiritual growth is ultimately about reasserting control in a part of your life that was yielded to the undisciplined part of your nature. Less control equals less happiness; more control equals more happiness. Therefore, to improve your experience of life, sow better seeds. You take control by the seeds that you sow.

Questions

1. What people or beings exist that you cannot see?

2. What places or realms exist that you cannot see?

3. What things or entities exist that you cannot see?

4. How do people know these beings, realms and entities exist?

5. What is faith, according to Hebrews 11:1?

6. How do you increase desirable qualities in your life?

7. Today's experiences are a composite of what?

8. When you cannot change your circumstances, what should you change?

9. In what unusual place did Paul rejoice?

10. What four words summarize the process of spiritual growth?

Discussion Questions

1. Why pray in the morning? noon? evening?

2. How is praying like getting dressed? How is it like running?

3. What are the limits of guilt and shame in producing spiritual growth?

Assignment

Seed of the Week: Thankfulness

When and where will you sow a small seed of thankfulness this week? The amount of joy you have in life will be in direct proportion to your gratitude. To have a better life, cultivate an appreciative life.

Weed of the Week: Ingratitude

The less grateful a person is, the less happy he is. Taking God's blessings for granted is like stealing. Not only do we rob God of the glory He deserves, but we rob ourselves of countless small pleasures.

Reflection and Prayer:

What do you reap when you sow more thankfulness and less discontent on a daily basis? Ask God to help you count your blessings this week and stop taking His goodness for granted.

CHAPTER 11

Sowing Seeds of RELATIONAL GROWTH
Improving My Relationships, One Seed at a Time

*"A person who sows seeds of kindness enjoys
a perpetual harvest."*
– Anonymous

When John warned his readers not to love the world, he was making a statement about the values of believers in Christ. Money and material possessions have their use, but they are not primary sources of satisfaction or greatness. They are tools and not gods. What really matters is not earthly riches but enduring relationships.

Although relationships vary, the key to improving them is the same: Sow seeds of love, and they will grow. Are there exceptions to this rule? Sure, but it is the right thing to do regardless. In rare cases when love is not returned, you are made better for the effort (Romans 12:17-21). And if the relationship does not grow, your character will. Hating the hateful, on the other hand, is responsible for the ever-downward spiral of sin.

Unraveling the Mystery of the Ages

Rather than focusing on exceptions to this perfectly good rule, why not rejoice that you have the power to improve your relationships with most people? Complaining about difficult relationships does nothing to improve them. Instead, it makes you feel helpless. By using the

Seed Principle, you have the ability to change things for the better. Remember Paul's promise:

> Do not be deceived, God is not mocked; for whatever a man sows, that he will also reap. For he who sows to his flesh will of the flesh reap corruption, but he who sows to the Spirit will of the Spirit reap everlasting life. And let us not grow weary while doing good, for in due season we shall reap if we do not lose heart. Therefore, as we have opportunity, let us do good to all, especially to those who are of the household of faith (Galatians 6:7-10).

The point is, if you are not getting the results you want, try something different. Paul knew that humans are prone to deceive themselves in this matter. When a relationship is not working, most people act mystified. They pretend they played no part in creating the tension that exists and that the other person's behavior is incomprehensible.

In most cases these people are reaping precisely what they have sown. When people sow to the flesh (jealousy, envy, selfishness, disrespect, criticism, manipulation), they damage or "corrupt" the relationship. When the relationship suffers, communication becomes difficult and detachment grows. Ties may be polite but distant or heated and destructive. In either case, little closeness exists. And unless they reverse course, the relationship will break down completely.

What is the answer to this mess? Do not despair – do good! Paul advised his readers not to give in to emotional weariness and withdraw from people who disappoint or perplex. Instead of giving up on the relationship, be on the lookout for opportunities to demonstrate love and do good. Sow to the Spirit, and see what happens. In due season, things will change for the better if you do not disengage. Why is that? Because everything brings forth after its kind. By returning good for evil, you can break the pattern of hurtful words and actions (Romans 12:17). Do not be deceived. Most of the time, you provoke the reaction you get; or as Paul put it, you reap what you sow. The sooner you get out of denial on this point, the sooner you can begin enjoying better relationships.

Growing Your Marriage

If you are not satisfied with your marriage relationship, the least helpful thing is to blame your mate for depriving you of the happiness you think you deserve (Genesis 3:12). You deceive yourself when you fail to see that you contributed to the problem. Or as Jesus put it, remove the log from your own eye before trying to remove the speck from your spouse's eye (Matthew 7:5). The first and best step to improving marital satisfaction is to look for constructive changes you can make in your own thinking and behavior.

Unfortunately, the typical response to an unhappy home life is to sow more of the same seeds that got you in trouble in the first place. In doing so, you perpetuate the problem you claim to want to solve. For instance, nagging does nothing to endear partners to each other. Instead it causes bitterness, which leads to withdrawal or reprisal. Solomon wrote extensively about the negative emotions produced by this irritating habit:

> Better to dwell in a corner of a housetop, than in a house shared with a contentious woman (Proverbs 21:9).

> A continual dripping on a very rainy day and a contentious woman are alike; whoever restrains her restrains the wind, and grasps oil with his right hand (Proverbs 27:15-16).

Even when criticism is justified, the wrong tone or attitude can damage a relationship. The information, although true, is not welcome. Rather than producing repentance, it can spark resentment and resistance. Whether you actively punish someone's bad behavior through anger and intimidation, or passively punish them through playing the martyr or turning a cold shoulder, you are sowing seeds of destruction in your marriage. You are provoking a reaction and then complaining about what you helped to create.

Sow Strategically

The key to a thriving marriage is to learn to sow more wisely. Keep in mind the harvest you desire. What do you want *for* your mate? Growth? Contentment? Joy? What do you need *from* your mate? Greater respect? More responsibility? Increased affection? Raging romance?

Once you know what it is, you are in a perfect position to steer the relationship in a new direction. Just sow the seeds that are likely to bring your vision to fruition.

For instance, a man who feels a need for more physical intimacy can try demanding it as a legal and spiritual right, but his efforts will not produce a willing, enthusiastic partner. A wiser man will employ his powers of investigation and imagination to discover the seeds of feminine desire. Loving requires learning. What makes her feel more amorous? Maybe it is more than roses and restaurants. Perhaps what she wants is uninterrupted conversation, or help with the dishes, or to watch you spend time with the kids. What dampens her desire? Is it fatigue, poor hygiene, bad timing, or lack of attention for her physical needs? Part of the fun of marriage is finding out what makes the other person tick. Sadly, all some people do is ask, "What have you done for me lately?" They make selfish demands based on thinking that fails to consider the future or the feelings of others.

Sow Charitably

The most important seeds you can sow in any relationship are seeds of love. Love occurs when you care enough about another's well-being to stretch yourself to meet his or her needs. The greatest of those needs is for spiritual growth: the increased capacity to love like God.

But what does it mean to love in a practical sense? It means valuing someone. When you love a pet, possession or pastime, you give it your attention and energy. As a result, you play with your Pekingese in the park, pamper your Pontiac GTO, or prune your prized flowers. Because they are valued, caring for them is not burdensome.

When you pay attention to your mate, it reveals that she is truly important to you. Attending to the needs of your spouse begins with taking time for her. That can mean scheduling date nights, exercising together, or getting away for a weekend. It may mean admiring her across a room or delighting in thoughts of her while you are apart. Regardless of proximity, she is present in your heart.

Listen to Love

Nothing says "I love you" like attentive listening. Conversely, nothing says "You are unimportant to me" like ignoring her or dismissing her words lightly. When you see your mate as an inferior person who exists only to serve your needs, you take little interest in her thoughts, feelings and aspirations. But when you care for her as an equal who completes you with her insights, you hunger to hear more about her passion and perspective.

Loving means enjoying what makes your mate unique as a human being. That does not mean glorifying or excusing character flaws, but it does mean appreciating differences (opinions, priorities and interests). Rather than punishing her for expressing herself, you encourage her to fulfill her dreams and her potential. When you help her become the best person she can be, your love grows as she grows.

When you begin to love your partner the way Christ loved the church, it gets easier to identify the seeds that will produce a successful marriage. Jesus saw the church's needs and sacrificed to meet them because His heart inclined Him to do so. When your heart disposes you to deny yourself for your spouse's well-being, you are starting to understand your Savior's love. When you lay down your life so that she may have a more abundant life, you are practicing true love.

Love can be revealed by words, but it is authenticated by deeds (1 John 3:7, 10, 18). When these conflict, the simplest action trumps the strongest emotion. In the end, love is what love does. Love is paying bills, sharing meals, comforting fears and drying tears.

Growing Your Children

Wise parents use the Seed Principle in their practice of parenting. They envision the people of faith and character their children can become and sow to that end. They are intentional and tactical rather than emotional and erratic. They anticipate what their words and actions are likely to produce, and focus on results rather than approval. Through word and deed, they promote lives of faith, hope and love. They model self-management and consideration of others. They create opportunities for children to develop virtue and ask lots of questions to increase their powers of discernment.

In brief, loving parents provide their children with four essentials for healthy growth: education, example, experience and encouragement. For example, if I want my children to be fiscally responsible, I must teach them the principles of money management, demonstrate monetary discipline in my own life, provide age-appropriate opportunities to handle money, and supply supportive accountability. Assuming children will learn life lessons on their own leaves them at the mercy of unreliable information and deprives them of the reinforcement they need to build good habits.

When a baby is born, God intends to accomplish two things: Establish a safe environment where the child can mature and provide a challenging environment where the parents can grow. Helping another human being learn the ropes of life is a sobering responsibility. When Junior arrives, mom and dad are forced to reevaluate their beliefs and values. In caring for a son or daughter, parents must come to terms with the meaning of life and the basis of happiness. So, as parents mold their children, God is busy molding parents.

Growing Your Friendships

Genuine friendship is a rare and rewarding experience. A friend is a kindred spirit for whom you feel regard as well as affection. Mutual respect (not mutual indulgence) is the foundation of friendship. The relationship grows as you get to know a person, like him, and trust him to do you good and not harm. He is more than a chum or crony. A faithful friend is part colleague, coach and collaborator in the business of life.

In today's world, much passes for friendship that is exploitation or parasitism. One who asks you to do something illegal, immoral or unethical is a foe rather than a friend. When a relationship depletes your spiritual vitality, something evil is present. However, no one can diminish your spirit without your cooperation (James 1:14).

Ask yourself: Does this relationship bring out the best in me?
• Does it make me feel stronger and more spiritual?
• Does it encourage and empower me?
• Does it challenge and stretch me?

If the answer is no, you have an acquaintance at best and an enemy at worst – but definitely not a friend. If a relationship fails to ennoble and inspire you but does you no harm, you have made an acquaintance. If a relationship drags you down and diminishes your soul, you have discovered a foe. Despite anything he says to the contrary, he is an adversary and not an ally.

Three Seeds of Lasting Friendship

Making friends involves responsibility as well as chemistry. To cultivate a friendship you must take the initiative by showing yourself friendly (Proverbs 18:24). Rather than wondering why others are unsociable, you should ask what you might be doing to keep them at a distance. Three seeds must be sown by a person to be friend-worthy.

• **Honesty.** The first seed is honesty (Ephesians 4:25). Friends do not wear masks around each other. If you cannot be yourself and say what you think, no closeness really exists. Solomon said, "Faithful are the wounds of a friend, but the kisses of an enemy are deceitful" (Proverbs 27:6). Enemies tell you what they think you want to hear. Their aim is to please you rather than improve you. If you have an associate who never disagrees with you, watch out. A word of warning before leaving this subject: Do not bare your soul to just anyone. Friendships develop over time, and self-revelation should occur on a gradual basis.

• **Curiosity.** The second seed you must sow to develop a friendship is curiosity. In addition to revealing yourself, you must show an interest in the other person. Some people use their friends to satisfy their own egos. Healthy relationships bring about a desire to explore the personality of the other. When you know what makes someone laugh or cry, you are forming the basis of a friendship. When you know someone's hopes and dreams, you are bonding on a deeper level. Associates transact business, but friends touch each other's hearts and transform each other's lives. "As iron sharpens iron, so a man sharpens the countenance of his friend" (Proverbs 27:17).

• **Loyalty.** The third seed is loyalty. Friends are honorable people. They are safe to be around. They keep your confidences, guard your reputation, and look out for your interests. They will not abandon you in time of difficulty. Indeed, "A friend loves at all times" (Proverbs 17:17).

The Seed of Presence

Life's most precious moments are often unplanned. You just have to be there at the right time. Therefore, if you want to improve a relationship with someone, spend more time with that person. Presence is critical because it is hard to script moments of bliss. They are joyous precisely because they are surprising. If we had foreseen them, they would not have touched us in the same way.

A bonding experience is as indescribable as it is spontaneous. Those who were absent at the critical moment find it impossible to appreciate what took place. It involves a soul connection that reaches beyond ordinary experience. That tie is reflected in the closeness between David and Jonathan, Paul and Timothy, and Aquila and Priscilla. Hearts are knit together in mutual joy and respect.

Enduring romances and satisfying friendships have a comfortable, relaxed feel to them. You can let down your hair and your guard. They involve moments that are unhurried and free of care. They allow you to be yourself and your best. The same is true in your relationship with the Lord.

The Ultimate Test

The goal of every relationship should be to contribute something of value to another's life (Galatians 6:10). Whether that person is your spouse, child, friend or co-worker, ask yourself, "Are they better off for knowing me?" Relationships are God's tools for molding and shaping people. They are intended to draw out potential and support growth.

Choosing a marriage partner, close friend or business partner is not as difficult as many believe, but it does require honesty. Ask yourself, "Is this person bringing out the best in me?" Those closest to you may be able to assess the situation better than you can. If you have the courage to ask, they will tell you things you cannot see because of your emotional entanglement. If they see you headed for a train wreck, pay attention. Realize that everyone – including you – has blind spots that hinder objectivity. Get your head out of the sand, and read the signs. Ask, "Is this relationship doing both of us good?"

No relationship is easy, but without relationships, life is positively barren. In most cases they reflect back to you something about yourself and your choices. Do not despair if you are in the midst of relational difficulties. Just make up your mind to sow different seeds to enjoy sweeter fruit. Ask yourself, "What is this relationship trying to teach me about myself?" The quicker you learn the lesson, the faster you and the relationship can improve.

Most of all, make up your mind that you will be a blessing to all whom you meet (Genesis 12:3). Are people changed for the better because of your contagious smile, words of encouragement and comforting presence? May the seeds you plant in the souls around you bear pleasant fruit that improves the world and gladdens the heart of God.

FOR GOOD

I've heard it said
That people come into our lives for a reason
Bringing something we must learn
And we are led
To those who help us most to grow
If we let them
And we help them in return
Well, I don't know if I believe that's true
But I know I'm who I am today
Because I knew you
Like a comet pulled from orbit
As it passes a sun
Like a stream that meets a boulder
Halfway through the wood
Who can say if I've been changed for the better?
But because I knew you
I have been changed for good

– Stephen Schwartz, musical theater composer

Questions

1. What did John say Christians should not love?

2. Next to God, what should Christians love most?

3. What is the key to improving any relationship?

4. What is responsible for the ever-downward spiral of sin?

5. What should you consider doing when a relationship is not working?

6. What is the least helpful thing you can do for a troubled marriage?

7. What is the most helpful thing you can do to improve your marriage?

8. What does it mean to love in a practical sense?

9. What are you saying to people when you do not listen to them?

10. What is the goal of every relationship?

Discussion Questions

1. What is the difference between primary and secondary greatness?

2. What do you want for your mate? What seeds should you sow?

3. Why is spending time together important for improving relationships?

Assignment

Seed of the Week: Hope

When and where will you sow a small seed of hope this week? Hope is the spiritual energy that motivates positive action. When you express confidence in others, it helps them to believe in themselves. Love hopes all things (1 Corinthians 13:7).

Weed of the Week: Despair

When you feel hopeless, you are not thinking clearly. It means you are relying too much on yourself and not enough on God. Faith in God's presence and promises produces holy optimism even in the midst of great difficulties.

Reflection and Prayer:

What do you reap when you sow more hope and less gloom on a daily basis? Ask God to help you become more upbeat and less downcast this week.

CHAPTER 12

Sowing Seeds of ORGANIZATIONAL GROWTH

Improving My Influence, One Seed at a Time

"You have to sow before you can reap.
You have to give before you can get."
– Robert Collier, author

Organizational growth depends on personal growth. To accomplish bigger goals, you must first become a bigger person. Then an additional layer of leadership skills must be added to improve the performance of your team, increase the profits of your company, or grow the attendance of your local church.

To illustrate this point, look below at the ascending scale of human needs that are satisfied by the progressive awakening of the soul. When you are physically, socially, mentally and spiritually healthy, you are in a better position to lead others than one who is severely lacking in any of these areas.

1. **PHYSICAL NEEDS**
   a. Areas of concern: Existence and security
   b. Result when met: Wellness of the body
   c. Feelings produced: I am safe and sound.

2. **SOCIAL NEEDS**
   a. Areas of concern: Family and community
   b. Result when met: Wellness of the heart
   c. Feelings produced: I am loved and supported.

3. **MENTAL NEEDS**
   a. Areas of concern: Identity and efficacy
   b. Result when met: Wellness of the mind
   c. Feelings produced: I am responsible and capable.

4. **SPIRITUAL NEEDS**
   a. Areas of concern: Integrity and empathy
   b. Result when met: Wellness of the soul
   c. Feelings produced: I am whole and loving.

A leader takes this hierarchy of human needs and applies them to a larger setting. But before he can influence another person, he must climb the ladder of personal growth himself. When a person in a leadership position is physically deprived, socially disconnected, mentally deluded or spiritually divided, he is too needy himself to care for others. His immaturity and imbalance pervert his perspective and preoccupy his mind. When a person feels safe, supported, strong and spiritually centered, he can devote his attention to larger concerns than self. His wholeness can be placed in service to those he loves.

A leader has earned the right of influence by traveling the hard road of change ahead of his followers. By going first he is positioned to assist them in journeying to life's next significant milestone. He does not have to be faultless, but he must go before his followers in three significant ways.

Become a Bigger Person

The first step in organizational growth is to become a bigger person. A good way to do this is to make and follow a personal growth plan. A balanced plan has two focus areas: character (who you are) and competence (what you do). Personal integrity and specialized ability are both necessary to living your best life. However, a comprehensive plan also should encourage growth in well-rounded living. Four primary concerns are your faith, family, fitness and finances. The healthier you become, the more you can contribute to others.

Assess Your Need

A good plan begins by assessing your present status in areas where you choose to concentrate your efforts. A scale of one (lowest) to 10 (highest) can be used to quantify your satisfaction in these life accounts. This scale is simple but broad enough to measure incremental growth – the most typical, realistic and positive kind. What would it look and feel like if you rated yourself a 10 in any of these areas? The more detail you add to this picture, the more motivational your goal becomes. By visualizing, verbalizing and emotionalizing your goals, the probability of reaching them increases dramatically. See it, say it and sense it.

Chart Your Path

When you see your target clearly and assess your situation accurately, you are prepared to plot a path to improved performance. Ask yourself, "What is the next faithful step to move me forward in my journey to greater happiness and usefulness?" Identify and prioritize new action steps. Anticipate obstacles and prepare contingency plans. Identify relationships and resources you will need to achieve your objective. Then determine how you must change in order to be equal to the task.

Five areas of personal growth are critical for larger success. Effective leaders are committed to growth in knowledge, integrity, commitment, gratitude and initiative. A quick review of these components will help you see how each contributes to the success of your team.

1. Increase Your Knowledge

To illustrate the way personal growth is connected to organizational growth, imagine your dream is to grow a local church. To accomplish your goal you must increase your knowledge in your chosen field. Can you effectively communicate who Jesus is and how He saves people from their sins? Can you explain the reasonableness and attractiveness of the Christian faith to those harassed by doubt?

For example, many people struggle with the idea of hell. They ask, "If God is love (1 John 4:8), how could He possibly subject souls to endless suffering?" Faulty reasoning leads them to reject God or abandon His teaching about eternal punishment. In actuality, you cannot fully appreciate God's love without understanding His teaching about hell. Why allow His Son to be tortured if hell is not real and horrible? Did Jesus die for a figure of speech? Why then the thorns and nails and cries and agony? How is grace so amazing if hell is a mere analogy?

The fact is that God sends no one to hell, but He did send His Son to keep you out of hell. Hell is voluntary. Those who go there do so by choice despite everything God has done to deliver them. He has described the conditions of hell in the clearest possible terms (fire, darkness, separation, tears, gnashing of teeth). All that can be done without violating your free will has been done.

Studying God's Word allows you to go before others mentally to guide their thinking and lead them to faith in Christ. If you have not thought deeply about His teaching, you will lack the confidence and competence needed to capitalize on evangelistic opportunities that arise. Exhaustive knowledge is not necessary to begin evangelizing, but increased knowledge can help you do a better job of addressing the needs of potential converts.

2. Increase Your Integrity

Another critical factor in becoming an effective evangelist (or leader of any kind) is spiritual integrity. A man who lives a double life loses something vital in his ability to communicate the gospel, but authenticity helps a preacher deliver his message with intensity. A man who is unsure of his beliefs cannot preach with the same force as one who is deeply convicted. Unresolved doubts drain a Christian's confidence and lessen his will to invest himself wholly in his cause. Likewise, besetting sins distract an evangelist from his mission and deplete his spiritual energy. When hearers sense uncertainty or insincerity in a speaker's voice, they discount his words. On the other hand, when the soul-winner's heart is aligned with his purpose, the difference is unmistakable. His message is reinforced by an obvious tone of sincerity and vitality that speaks straight to the heart of the listener.

When Jesus declared, "I am the way, the truth and the life," He was inviting His followers to examine His conduct in the light of His teaching. Those who accepted Christ's challenge found Him to be a man of integrity. His life and message were one. Experienced leaders know that the most powerful influence any person has is his example. People do what people see. When they glimpse the fruit of the Spirit in the life of an evangelist, they listen with more interest. The presence of a soul-winner with an undivided heart is an amazing thing to witness.

Those who heard Jesus preach marveled because He spoke as one who had authority. The word "authority" refers to right or power. Your right to be heard is earned through disciplined living. Likewise, the impact of your message depends on the consistency between your words and conduct. Successful preachers and leaders demonstrate what they hope to cultivate.

3. Increase Your Commitment

The biggest obstacle to evangelizing the world is a shortage of commitment. Just think about it: If the money and manpower currently available in Jesus' church could be redirected to reach the lost, the results would be immediate and dramatic. Despite claims to the contrary, evangelism is not a top priority for many Christians.

Commitment moves a goal to the front of the line. It changes an idle dream into an urgent priority. Commitment elevates an objective to a place of higher importance. It devotes mental and physical energy to its accomplishment. It is a function of the will that focuses attention and effort on the heart's deepest desire.

All that stands between most people and the life of their dreams is commitment. So what do you want to have? do? become? How badly do you want it? Are you ready to pay the price? Are you prepared to stay the course? It is one thing to quote the Great Commission and quite another to commit to it body and soul.

When is the last time you went on a mission trip? How long have you agonized in prayer over a person you are trying to reach for the Lord? How many letters of encouragement have you written to your church's missionaries? When is the last time you graded a Bible correspondence course for a student in a Third World country? Have you ever looked into the eyes of someone you love and told him about your concern for his soul? What have you risked or sacrificed to share the gospel of Christ with another? And by the way, did you invite anyone to worship God with you this Sunday?

4. Increase Your Gratitude

The greatest motivation for commitment is gratitude. Christians love lost people because Jesus first loved them. His devotion to their needs stirs them to care for the needs of others. Jesus' forgiveness was the moving force behind Paul's ministry and the power behind Peter's preaching. It is the reason why moments of worship are so critical to Christian living. Those who take time to gather around the Lord's table leave there with a renewed appreciation for the depth of His love.

On the other hand, saints who spend hours surfing the Web but cannot find minutes for prayer will soon lose their commitment to Christ. And those who spend more time with remote in hand than Bible in hand should not be surprised when their love for souls grows icy cold. Gratitude produces commitment, and reflection is the seedbed of gratitude.

5. Increase Your Initiative

Make no mistake: Commitment is about action and not just emotion. It must be expressed and not merely felt. You cannot hide what you think about every day and dream about every night. Lukewarm faith needs no outlet, but fervent faith must find a release or it will rupture the soul. Depression, disease and death often are symptoms of a soul that was denied its calling. Spinelessness and slothfulness betray the soul's greatness. Playing it safe and settling for mediocrity are cowardly acts. Constructively challenging the status quo and striving to make things better are the Christian way. Hirelings are never heroes because they lack the fortitude to stay the course when times get hard. Commitment is not flashy or flamboyant. It is about grit and guts and doing whatever it takes to get the job done.

According to the Seed Principle, life has a divine order that must be followed to experience long-term success. Before there is a return, there must be a risk. Before there is a harvest, there must be a seed. Before there is victory, there must be a battle. So, how dedicated are you on a scale from one to 10? What would have to change to raise your level of devotion by a single point? What is holding you back from taking the next faithful step? If you ignore the summons of your soul, are you ready to live with less than your best? And are you prepared to explain your reasons to God at the judgment? Which would disappoint Him more: the person who gave his all and fell shy of his goal, or the person who lacked enough faith to try in the first place (Matthew 25:24-30)? The effort, not the outcome, determines faithfulness.

Create a Better Culture

Once you make a wholehearted commitment to personal and organizational growth, the Seed Principle will provide you with a simple strategy for accomplishing your dreams. Adopt a sower's attitude, and begin broadcasting small seeds that will result in a fruitful harvest over time. Think about every small improvement you can make as an investment in the future. The combination of those efforts will ultimately pay rich dividends. Your success will seldom hinge on one thing working perfectly. It is more likely to result from the culmination of many things working in harmony. Creating a culture or environment for growth is the most important thing leaders do.

• **Sow an uplifting physical environment.** Physical environments are a reflection of the inward condition of the groups using them. What messages do your surroundings send to visitors? What would you like them to say? Ask a trusted friend outside your group to give you three suggestions for improving your first impression and raising the morale of your members (e.g., eye-catching signage, colorful landscaping, fresh paint, bright lighting, attractive flooring, current bulletin boards, contemporary bathrooms, absence of clutter, etc.).

1. Rate your physical environment. 1 2 3 4 5 6 7 8 9 10 +

2. Name three things you would change if you had the power to do so.

3. What would others say is the highest priority item on your list?

4. How might you gain support to implement this change?

• **Sow a healthful spiritual environment.** Spiritual environments are the soil that supports healthy human growth. Does the atmosphere in your congregation bless or burden people? Does it help them live well or create dysfunction? Does it make them feel more resilient or stressed? Does it energize them or drain them dry?

1. Rate your spiritual environment. 1 2 3 4 5 6 7 8 9 10 +

2. Name three things you would change if you had the power to do so.

3. What would others say is the highest priority item on your list?

4. How might you gain support to implement this change?

• **Sow an encouraging relational environment.** Are people in your group close and well connected? What opportunities do you provide for strengthening relationships? Do your members share good times and support one another in difficult times? Are their ties deep and genuine or shallow and superficial?

1. Rate your relational environment. 1 2 3 4 5 6 7 8 9 10 +

2. Name three things you would change if you had the power to do so.

3. What would others say is the highest priority item on your list?

4. How might you gain support to implement this change?

• **Sow a decidedly inspirational environment.** If the gospel is good news, then its primary focus must be on that which is good. A steady diet of negativity is neither Christlike nor constructive. Perfectionism in the pulpit is a recipe for perpetual discouragement. Growth environments demand accountability but encourage progress along a pathway of personal growth.

1. Rate your positive environment. 1 2 3 4 5 6 7 8 9 10 +

2. Name three things you would change if you had the power to do so.

3. What would others say is the highest priority item on your list?

4. How might you gain support to implement this change?

• **Sow a challenging leadership environment.** A stream cannot rise higher than its source. Therefore, a strong commitment to leadership development is essential for long-term success. Does your organization have a concrete plan for equipping new leaders? Does it have a culture conducive to growing leaders?

1. Rate your leadership development culture. 1 2 3 4 5 6 7 8 9 10 +

2. Name three things you would change if you had the power to do so.

3. What would others say is the highest priority item on your list?

4. How might you gain support to implement this change?

Take Bolder Action

The third essential for organizational success is courageous action. Daring leaders sow continuously, bountifully and fervently to harvest their dreams.

Sow continuously by adopting an *improvement* mindset. There is no situation in life that cannot be improved for the better. All that is needed is a little imagination and enthusiasm. Seeing opportunities has more to do with your heart than head. Caring is the key to consistent progress.

Sow bountifully by adopting an *abundance* mindset. You can increase your probabilities of success by doing more than the minimum to reach your goals. Do more than is expected to add value to people and projects. Make excellence your reputation, and refuse to live life just getting by. Your return will reflect your effort.

Sow fervently by adopting a *confident* mindset. Success is guaranteed if you do not lose heart and give up. Optimism is the birthright of believers. Pessimism is the legacy of losers. When you sow confidently, rest assured that the harvest is on its way!

Where conversions are not occurring regularly, sowing is not occurring reliably. To counter that trend a comprehensive plan is needed to raise the soul consciousness of your congregation. No mere change in methodology will do. It will take a radical mental makeover to overcome the fearfulness and laziness that inhabit people's hearts.

The key is to focus attention and structure effort toward caring for the most precious thing on earth: souls (Matthew 16:26). Because a soul is the most valuable thing on earth, caring for them must be the most important work on earth. It is the reason for the church's existence. God forbid that it should ever become an inconvenience or interruption.

In the garden of Gethsemane, Jesus instructed His disciples to watch and pray. When souls are not being saved, there is a lack of watching and praying for opportunities to share Christ. Imagine standing before the Lord one day and telling Him, "I'm sorry I never introduced anyone to you, but I never got the chance to share the gospel." Jesus said the fields are white unto harvest. The key is to see people through His eyes. More love equals more souls liberated from sin. Those who watch for Jesus' return are more likely to watch out for their fellow man.

Invisible Souls

Jesus once told a story about a selfish man who awoke in torment after he died (Luke 16:19-31). During his lifetime he was clothed in purple and fine linen and feasted sumptuously every day. But while he indulged himself, a poor man named Lazarus lay begging at his gate. Covered with sores from undernourishment, Lazarus longed to be fed with the crumbs that fell from the rich man's table, but to no avail.

When reading this disturbing account, we find ourselves repulsed by the insensitivity of a man who could ignore such intense suffering by another soul. Did he not see him? Did he not care? We consider the rich man's punishment just for his heartless crime.

But to borrow from the words of Nathan the prophet, "Are you the man?" (2 Samuel 12:7). As a Christian you are wealthy beyond imagination (James 2:5). At your conversion you were clothed with Christ (Galatians 3:26-27), and now you feast lavishly upon God's Word as often as you like (Matthew 4:4). While you enjoy these generous blessings, others go wanting. They are impoverished by their lack of knowledge and plagued by festering sins, the result of spiritual malnutrition. Like unclean dogs licking the wounds of Lazarus, unbelievers attempt to heal the pain of sinners with failed philosophies and false religions.

But every day, God lays someone at your gate – someone whose soul yearns to be fed with the crumbs of your faith in Christ. Do you walk right past him in your school, on your street, or at your workplace? Do you share even one morsel of the gospel with the neediest of this world – the lost? If not, why not? Could it be that you do not share because you do not care? Blindness is an ailment of the heart and not just the eyes. To love more is to see more and to save more.

Sowing Single-Mindedly

Of all the people you meet, 100 percent possess an immortal soul. Saving those souls is the responsibility of 100 percent of God's people. And watching for soul-saving opportunities should fill 100 percent of a Christian's waking hours. Soul consciousness is essential for the business of evangelism to succeed. Those who sow continuously, bountifully and fervently will find their efforts blessed.

The salvation of one soul is worth 100 "no's" in the course of broadcasting the gracious invitation of Christ. When the seed of God's kingdom is received by a single good-hearted soul, it will reproduce itself 30-, 60- or 100-fold in time to come (Mark 4:8). With this assurance, faithful sowers go about their business with confidence in the power of God's Word to fulfill its purpose. Those who sow single-mindedly will reap a bountiful harvest in keeping with their faith and industry.

A Quick Review

Be it a church, company or club, the same essentials are needed to improve your team's productivity:

- Become a bigger person.
- Create a better culture.
- Take bolder action.

To become a bigger person, seek improvement in five areas: your knowledge, integrity, commitment, gratitude and initiative. Self-development is critical for lasting organizational success. When hypocrisy and complacency rule the day, trouble is sure to follow. Make a commitment to work as hard on yourself as you do on your job.

To create a better culture, model an attitude of continuous improvement for your team. The key to success is to think small and focus on incremental improvements in all parts of your organization. Growth environments encourage feedback and embrace change. When good and noble hearts unite, the future is always bright.

To take bolder action, three tactical steps are needed: You must sow consistently, abundantly and fervently. Conversely, those who sow infrequently, sparsely and timidly can expect meager results. The secret to success is sowing more of what you want. In due season your dedication is sure to be rewarded. You have God's Word on it.

Questions

1. What must a person do to accomplish bigger goals?

2. What happens when a leader is deprived, disconnected, delusional or divided?

3. What happens when he feels safe, supported, strong and spiritually centered?

4. How does a leader earn the right to influence others?

5. Name two things a personal growth plan should address.

6. How do besetting sins undermine the work of evangelists?

7. What is the best way to influence others?

8. What is the biggest obstacle to world evangelism?

9. What is the greatest motivation for commitment?

10. Name three tactics for sowing more success.

Discussion Questions

1. Why is integrity essential for success?

2. Why is commitment crucial for success?

3. How can thinking small help you achieve your dreams?

Assignment

Seed of the Week: Forgiveness

When and where will you sow a small seed of forgiveness this week? Forgiveness is the highest form of love known to man. When you have been wounded by another, you are faced with the most important choice of your life. Will you extend mercy or perpetuate misery?

Weed of the Week: Resentment

Grudges are like unsightly, unmanageable crabgrass in the flowerbed of the soul. A bitter life can never be a beautiful life. Rid your heart of resentment, and start enjoying more health and happiness today.

Reflection and Prayer:

What do you reap when you sow more forgiveness and less resentment on a daily basis? Ask God to help you become more gracious and less grudging this week.

CHAPTER 13

The Sower's
ALMANAC
Forecasting Success

"If seeds in the black earth can turn into such beautiful roses,
what might not the heart of man become
in its long journey toward the stars?"
– English writer G.K. Chesterton

Jesus chose three images to illustrate the major obstacles that keep people from enjoying the results (harvest) they want in life:

- **A hard path:** A dismissive attitude that overlooks dangers and opportunities

- **A hidden rock:** A limiting belief that blocks the way to long-term growth and success

- **A hurtful thorn:** A competing interest that diverts attention from a primary purpose

Conversely, three things are necessary to achieve success in any undertaking. Those essentials are faith, follow-through and focus. When you believe in something fervently, commit to it fully and attend it faithfully, the likelihood of success is vastly increased. And although a particular goal may go unfulfilled, you will succeed in something far more important: living a courageous, God-honoring life.

Faith

According to Hebrews 11:1, faith is about hope fulfillment. Faith is the spiritual link to the life you want to live and the difference you hope to make in the world. As a preacher I spend my days trying to convince people that God's Word will help them fulfill their legitimate needs and deepest desires. Take some time today to think about your dreams for the future. Ask yourself, "How can faith help me overcome the obstacles that stand between me and what I want?"

If you desire the right things for the right reasons, God will come to your aid (James 4:1-3). He wants you to be with Him in heaven for eternity (1 Timothy 2:3-4), and He wants you to have the best possible life on earth (John 10:10). If He made a planet for you, formed a body for you, gave His Son for you, sent His Spirit to assist you, wrote the Bible to guide you, established His church to support you, and prepared heaven to reward you, don't you think He cares about your hopes and dreams? Trust that He loves you, hears the cries of your heart, and works on your behalf. With a little faith (Matthew 17:20) and a lot of patience (Galatians 6:9), your dreams really can come true (Ephesians 3:20).

Faith is what is needed to move from the wayside to the winning side of life. It can transform a timid mindset into one of steely confidence. If you are tired of having your dreams trampled by the cynicism of others, you need faith. If you are weary of seeing your desires swallowed by doubt, you need faith. There is no shortage of those who would crush your hope and douse your zeal, but faith is the shield that protects what is most precious in life (Ephesians 6:16). Belief in your God, your vision and yourself are essential to success. To achieve worthy aims, you must deeply, thoroughly and passionately believe.

Blind faith that ignores life's realities is a fraud. It must be pampered and protected to survive. It is constructed of fears, prejudices and wishful thinking. Make-believe faith cowers in the darkness of denial and self-deception. Genuine faith faces facts bravely. It does not have to be shielded from the truth. Legitimate faith lives in the light of full and honest examination.

Follow-Through

When I think about the benefits of endurance, I am reminded of a trip I took with my wife, Lisa. It started with a visit to see our grandchildren, Luke and Abby. During our brief stay, we were able to see Luke play T-ball in his inaugural season. It brought back memories of tossing the ball around with his dad, Buddy. Every day when I came home from work, we practiced. But more important than developing athletic skills was watching him grow in self-assurance born of hard work. One pitch and catch at a time, he was growing in confidence that he was equal to the game of life.

From Cookeville, Tenn., we headed off to Springfield, Mo., to preach a gospel meeting for the Water Mill Church of Christ. We decided to take a northerly route and traveled Interstate 24 to Paducah, Ky., before taking Highway 60 across Missouri. We ate supper at Lake Barkley Lodge and were shocked by the number of fallen trees we saw in the park. I asked the cashier at the restaurant what had happened. He told me they had suffered their worst ice storm on record and had been without power for weeks. From Paducah to Poplar Bluff, I was astonished to see the devastation to the landscape. It had an eerie look like the aftermath of a nuclear holocaust. The folks in Springfield told me they had suffered something similar a few years earlier, and then I was even more amazed at the earth's ability to heal itself over time.

On Friday after the meeting concluded, I was about to learn a lesson in humility as well as perseverance. We made it to Nashville and ate our pasta pre-race meal in preparation for the Country Music Marathon. It turned out to be the hottest day in the event's 10-year history with most people walking part of the way (including four miles for yours truly). One of my favorite things to do when running a marathon is to read the T-shirts of fellow participants. Some of my favorites were, "Who moved the finish line?" and "What was I thinking?" But top honors go to a lady with a shirt that said, "I'm a completer, not a competer." On this balmy day, Lisa finished walking her first half-marathon in three and a half hours, 15 minutes under the time limit required to receive a participant's medal. And by the way, her sugar levels are the best they have been since she was first diagnosed with diabetes 10 years ago. I hit a wall at 18 and a half miles and thought I was done. Somehow I kept going and revived a couple of miles later.

I am no athlete, but it does me good to stretch my legs and breathe deeply. It also does something for my soul to struggle to the finish line when I think I have nothing left to give. It reminds me that perseverance is the magic of life. Just hang in there, and wonderful things happen.

Children grow, landscapes heal, runners medal and churches blossom. When you feel like giving up, remember these words from Hebrews 12:1: "Therefore we also, since we are surrounded by so great a cloud of witnesses, let us lay aside every weight, and the sin which so easily ensnares us, and let us run with endurance the race that is set before us."

Before you bail on your goals and dreams, ask yourself, "What might be waiting for me if I hang in there just a little longer?" Just around the corner of your pain and discouragement is where you find the good stuff in life. That is where graduations, golden anniversaries and eternal glory can be found. Go slow if you must, and crawl if you have to, but press on (Philippians 3:14).

Stress is to people what sunshine is to plants. It forces them to grow or die. It demands that they stretch to meet the needs of the occasion or shrivel under the strain of their doubts and fears. One way or the other, stress is a call for change. Those who grow inwardly benefit from life's pressures. Those who ignore life's call for change suffer physically, emotionally and spiritually. The pain of growth is substantial, but the price of not growing is profoundly greater.

Abundant life is not a carefree life; rather, it is learning how to handle daily pressures in beneficial ways. It is not a life of perfection but of growth. The inability to process stress responsibly is a spiritual problem at its roots. Sin is the result of choosing selfish, short-sighted responses to life's problems. Shallowness of this kind is more than a psychological malady. It is sinful because it reflects an unwillingness to trust God. By ignoring His words and attempting our own solutions, we hurt those around us in hope of sparing ourselves pain. It is a cowardly choice that dishonors God and devastates others. Sinful lives are made of cowardly choices prompted by doubt, fear and selfishness. Abundant lives are composed of courageous choices motivated by faith, hope and love.

Focus

The third element of a success mindset is attentiveness. The ability to concentrate on things that matter is crucial for realizing your dreams. Attention is something that you invest. It is the ultimate currency of life. How you spend it is a reflection of what you consider important.

Because attention is limited, it reveals what you care about most. The key to living life at its best is balancing your focus in three areas: relationships, goals and values.

Relationships

Every life is made up of a hierarchy of relationships. Although all people possess worth and deserve respect, time cannot be evenly distributed among all living persons – not even the few who cross our paths. Courtesy is a debt owed to all, but attention is a gift bestowed on few.

Priority 1: Your Relationship With God

On the top rung of the attention ladder is God. The Lord demands to be first in the lives of His followers and will not accept a backseat to anyone. This insistence on preeminence is not because of pride but propriety. As man's creator, redeemer and sustainer, only God is worthy of this kind of devotion. He alone is perfect in knowledge, power, holiness and love.

To put a flawed, perishable creature above your faultless, incorruptible Maker is a mistake of enormous proportions. This ingratitude manifests itself in confused beliefs, corrupt ethics and compromised relations. Without God at the center, life lacks proper order and harmony. To protect you from the harmful effects of pride, God asks for the first day of your week, the first fruits of your increase, and the first place in your heart. These requirements are not the selfish demands of an egocentric God, but the soul-centering strategies of a loving Father.

Priority 2: Your Relationship With Your Mate

On the second step of the attention ladder comes your mate. When a man and woman marry, they enter a covenant relationship founded on being the exclusive caregiver for one another's sexual needs and the primary provider of each other's material and emotional needs. When a spouse becomes preoccupied by a third party, a breach of contract has occurred. The neglected partner is deprived of what is due, and the marriage is destabilized. Although society is indifferent to such heartlessness, God leaves no doubt about His displeasure (Malachi 2:11-16).

And yet many who never strayed from their marriage have betrayed their vows by abusing or neglecting the one they promised to love and cherish until death. Ask yourself, "How cherished does my mate feel today?" If your spouse does not feel appreciated and adored, what seeds can you sow to change that impression? Your job is to find out what makes your partner feel treasured and to provide it. Let there be no doubt in your mate's mind that he or she occupies a place of unrivaled devotion second only to the Lord Himself.

Priority 3: Your Relationship With Your Children

Next to the Lord and your spouse, your children deserve your highest level of attention. Tending small children occupies a great deal of time, but there should be no doubt about the priority of the marital relationship. This should be evident in the honor and consideration you give your mate and your insistence that all family members do likewise. A reasonable bedtime for little ones leaves time for adult interaction and communicates the specialness of this higher bond. The greatest security a child knows is the stability of his home and his parents' devotion to one another.

When business and pleasure continually encroach on family time, danger ensues. The child's need for attention will be met one way or the other. Risky and socially inappropriate behaviors are cries for attention. According to Malachi, one job of spiritual leaders is to remind fathers to turn their hearts back to their children (Malachi 4:6). As children grow, they should not be entertained or indulged every waking hour, but interest in their affairs and dedication to their training should come before lesser commitments.

Keeping Your Sanity

After apportioning time to commune with God and care for your family, the remainder must be divided among church, extended family, friends, neighbors, co-workers, community, and those in need (widows, orphans, the poor, handicapped, elderly and infirm). Maintaining health and sanity in the midst of so many appeals for attention is no small task.

Luke wrote that Jesus "went about doing good" (Acts 10:38). The hardest part of doing good is pausing to consider what needs to be done. Opportunities abound, but the ability to recognize them is rare.

We must see them to seize them, but our minds are so preoccupied that opportunities go unnoticed.

Perhaps one solution takes into account our human condition. While you work on becoming more mindful and spontaneous in your charity, do not overlook the value of good old-fashioned habits. We use them every day to care for our bodies when we brush and floss our teeth. Could we not use them to care for our relationships and souls? What personal habits and family traditions could help make generosity second nature?

- Save your change every day for a year to support a good work you cherish. Put a medium-sized food storage container in your dressing area so you can toss coins in as you empty your pockets or purse. No borrowing – it's not yours anymore (actually, it never was).

- At least once a month, take the kids to visit a nursing home before worship on Sunday morning. When the children are grown, you won't remember the "lost" hour of sleep, and you surely will be proud of the way they think about others more than themselves.

- Build holiday traditions with different family members. Don't wait each year to figure out when everyone wants to get together. Set it in stone to save time, energy and confusion.

- Give your used car to a family in need rather than trade it in. It will make more of a difference to them than to you. Having no car payment can be a financial game-changer.

- Start a supper club with people you want to get to know. Provide the address and dress code and nothing more. All can use a little adventure in their lives.

- Secretly adopt an elderly friend, and remember him or her with cards, gifts or treats on special days.

- Buy season tickets to a theater or concert venue. It will give you regular date nights without having to stop and plan.

- Take the first three minutes after Sunday morning worship to greet visitors, and invite them to join you for lunch at a restaurant or your home.

- Invite old friends to your house for dessert after evening service, or head to a local coffee shop to savor a rich blend of Christian fellowship.

- Use email distribution lists to stay in touch with family and friends. It may not be as personal as you would like, but it's better than good intentions unfulfilled.

- Start a weekly or monthly staff lunch with colleagues from work, and don't talk business.

- Be your own scholarship fund, and pay a struggling student's tuition one semester (anonymously if you can). It is a special joy to help someone who is helping herself.

- Keep a young couple's kids once a month so they can go on a date night. Remember when you were scraping by and couldn't afford a movie, meal and sitter?

Stop and make your own list, and choose one thing you will do this week. Involving family members in addressing others' needs models social responsibility while strengthening family ties. However, from time to time a crisis will arise that demands immediate attention that cannot be scheduled. The parable of the good Samaritan urges flexibility in such cases. Do not allow yourself to be manipulated by people whose "needs" are unreasonable and unquenchable, but be alert to providential opportunities to do good (Galatians 6:10; Hebrews 13:1-2).

Goals

God has structured life so that attention must be shifted between engaging people directly and pursuing goals that serve their needs indirectly. Worthy goals are always people-centered. For instance, one who pursues higher education should have more than reputation and riches in mind. Increasing your ability to provide for your family, care for the needy and serve society are excellent reasons for going back to school. Getting physically fit to be admired or feared is shallow, but increasing energy and longevity to invest it in relationships and meaningful work is commendable.

The challenge lies in managing goals that compete for your attention. By writing, ranking, posting and scheduling priorities, you place them in a framework that supports focus. Deadlines and evaluations revive concentration by establishing accountability. The aim is to set yourself up for success by directing the right amount of attention to a goal at the right time. Because of the limits of human attention, less is more when setting goals. Attempting too many things at the same time can be emotionally overwhelming and physically exhausting. Experience will teach you the number of initiatives you can undertake at any given time to maximize productivity in a balanced, sustainable, life-enriching way. When you sense that your health or relationships are suffering, pull some weeds and reprioritize. You will feel better, get more done, and protect what you prize most.

Values

Relationships and goals are only as safe as your values are strong. Values are the storm wall of your soul. When they fail, everything is lost. Marriages, friendships, reputations and careers can be swept away like buildings caught in a tidal surge. When values are intact, they are buttresses against the forces that would erode your integrity and security. By protecting your values, you protect the people and dreams you treasure most.

One key to maintaining strong values is social reinforcement (Ecclesiastes 4:9-11). Choosing a mate who shares your most cherished beliefs increases the likelihood of passing them down to the next generation (2 Corinthians 6:14-18). Choosing friends who share your moral convictions improves the probability you will honor them when pressured to do otherwise. Choosing a work environment that supports your devotion to family raises the odds you will put them first. Downplaying your susceptibility to social influences is intellectually dishonest. Selecting companions carelessly places your family and future at risk.

Following the "less is more" philosophy, I want to highlight three virtues that are essential for successful living. Every biblical ethic is important, but focusing on them all simultaneously is impossible. Keep these three at the forefront of your mind to reinforce your highest commitments:

- **Charity:** Love leads the list of values that safeguard people's souls.

- **Conviction:** Second only to love is devotion to God's Word, which reveals how love expresses itself in practical ways.

- **Courage:** Bravery is the final virtue on my short-list because knowing what to do is worthless without the boldness to remain firm in the face of pressure.

Blended together, these qualities form a threefold cord that can withstand the worst this world has to offer.

The Fruitful Life

Every year the congregation where I preach adopts a theme to help us coordinate our labors. One recent theme was "The Year of Fruitfulness." During that time I taught a class about "the fruitful life" to help members understand the dynamics of personal growth. We discussed what it takes to achieve real success and how to help others experience growth that is meaningful and enduring.

Christianity is a way of life characterized by constant growth (John 15:1-2). Moreover, Jesus provided a clear path for growth that includes all the tools and resources you will need. Your lifetime on earth is the season for growth. Death is the end of the growing season and the time for reaping what you have sown. What is judgment but a time to face the choices you have made over your lifespan?

The ultimate source of growth is your relationship with God. His Son provided a perfect model for growth, and His Spirit supplied a faultless manual for growth. Like seed, His Word imparts spiritual life and initiates beneficial change; like soil, His church supports your development by providing assistance and accountability in a safe environment.

However, despite all that God has done to make transformation possible, the final responsibility for creating a fruitful life rests with you. Growth of this kind is intentional rather than accidental. A person must want to grow and be willing to pay the price to grow. A humble, teachable spirit is needed to learn the lessons that will ripen into wisdom, and a trusting, obedient spirit is required to apply those lessons so they may ripen into maturity.

Along the road of spiritual development are countless challenges you must face to move forward. The birds and rocks and thorns will test your commitment and cannot be ignored. You must meet them head-on even though doing so can cause temporary distress and heartache.

All pain is not good, but suffering born of self-discipline in pursuit of a worthy goal is a sign of growth that yields joy in the end.

Most problems are opportunities for spiritual growth in disguise. The key is to recognize them as invitations to become a bigger person. Life's difficulties were designed to stretch your soul to new dimensions. Because adversity draws out human potential, it is an essential part of the growth process.

Those who understand the purpose of trials are best equipped to handle them. That is why believers shine under pressure. The faith of Jesus never blazed more brilliantly than when He hung on the cross, and the faith of Job never beamed more brightly than in his hour of loss (Luke 23:34; Job 13:15). Troublesome times are growth opportunities because they require added faith to overcome (Acts 14:22).

Paying Attention

Jesus concluded the parable of the sower with an unforgettable expression that went straight to the heart of His message: "He who has ears to hear, let him hear!" (Matthew 13:9). The word "hear" means to attend, perceive or heed. Jesus wanted His disciples to know that the secret of a life well lived is to pay attention.

Successful people notice more than others. They observe the way people react to them and alter their behavior appropriately. They recognize that effort always precedes results and develop a bias for action. One by one, they discern the laws of life and add them to their success tool kit.

Will you wander haplessly through life wondering why things don't go your way? Or will you study life and apply its unbreakable principles in practical and beneficial ways? The purpose of paying attention is to make better choices – to note what works and does not work, to adjust and advance in the fine art of living. Through greater awareness, commitment and focus, you can create a life of enduring significance and satisfaction. The time has arrived to wake up and grow up. The time has come to begin sowing the life of your dreams!

Tool Time

As this book draws to a close, I want to leave you with a practical tool for living the most fruitful life possible. The Bible is the authoritative, unabridged manual for harvesting the best possible life. Although nothing can take its place, I hope you will find the shortened guide at the end of this chapter to be a helpful review of the spiritual laws of sowing and reaping.

This tool will keep the seed-stealer from running off with the new knowledge you have gained from this book. It will help you practice these principles so your good intentions will not wilt under the pressure of a busy schedule. And it will encourage you to remove the thorns that deplete your desire for a better life. Using this tool will keep the birds and rocks and weeds from sidetracking your success.

And the more you use it, the more deeply the Seed Principle will take root in your heart. It will become:

- Your default lens for viewing the world around you.

- The natural way you size up opportunities and dangers.

- Your mental frame for making choices and pursuing goals.

Your days of being unaware, uncommitted and unfocused are coming to an end. Your days of faith, follow-through and focus are just beginning.

This tool consists of a simple set of questions to help you apply the life-changing lessons from the parable of the sower. These questions provide you with a quick summary of Jesus' teaching about the laws of fruitful living and the ground of human growth. By using this instrument faithfully, you will live more fruitfully.

The tool is called "The Sower's Almanac" (see page 167). An almanac is a publication containing a calendar with information about the movements of the sun and moon and their effects on the earth. Just as there are physical laws that allow scientists to predict sunrises and sunsets, so God's Word contains spiritual laws that let wise people see how their choices will affect their futures. Those laws have been distilled and collected in the decision-making tool you are about to receive.

An almanac is not designed to foretell every detail about the weather, but is incredibly accurate when it comes to the big picture (tides and seasons). Similarly, the Seed Principle cannot tell you everything you would like to know about your love life and career, but it can forecast success and failure with precision. Take a few minutes to review the tool, and keep it handy when a decision is looming. Over time, commit it to memory so you will be prepared for any emergency that arises.

My final prayer is that you will share these laws with your friends and family members. They will thank you for introducing them to the Master Gardener and the secrets of the sower, but their growth and success will be your real satisfaction. Then God will look down from heaven and smile as He sees another heart bearing fruit to His glory.

"Then I looked, and behold, a white cloud, and on the cloud sat One like the Son of Man, having on His head a golden crown, and in His hand a sharp sickle. And another angel came out of the temple, crying with a loud voice to Him who sat on the cloud, 'Thrust in Your sickle and reap, for the time has come for You to reap, for the harvest of the earth is ripe.' So He who sat on the cloud thrust in His sickle on the earth, and the earth was reaped."
(Revelation 14:14-16)

Questions

1. Name three images Jesus used to portray obstacles to growth.

2. Name three things that are essential for success.

3. According to Hebrews 11:1, what is one purpose of faith?

4. What will God do if you want the right things for the right reasons?

5. What is needed to move from the wayside of life to the winning side?

6. What is constructed of assumptions, prejudices, fears and fantasies?

7. What lives in the light of full and honest examination?

8. What is the storm wall of your soul?

9. Why are troublesome times opportunities for spiritual growth?

10. What is the purpose of paying attention?

Discussion Questions

1. What seeds can you sow to be a better mate, parent or friend.

2. Name three seeds you can sow to achieve one of your goals.

3. Name three values that will protect what is precious in your life.

Assignment

Seed of the Week: Bravery

When and where will you sow a small seed of bravery this week? A successful life is a life of action. Because action entails risk, courage is needed to seize life's opportunities and taste its sweetest fruits. When faced with a decision, remember that the bolder path is usually the best path.

Weed of the Week: Timidity

Do you find it difficult to tell others what you think? Are you afraid to pursue the career of your dreams? Are you constantly settling for less than you want because of your fears? Jesus said a mustard seed of faith can move mountains of doubt. Triumph over tentativeness by trusting God more.

Reflection and Prayer:

What do you reap when you sow more bravery and less timidity on a daily basis? Ask God to help you become bolder and less hesitant this week.

The Sower's Almanac
Focused Questions for a Fruitful Life

Seed questions sharpen vision.
1. What would you like to reap (have, do, or be)?
2. Why do you want this (list and rank reasons)?
3. How will it look and feel to succeed (be graphic)?
4. What seeds will it require (thoughts, words and deeds)?

Sower questions encourage action.
1. Do you accept full responsibility for your garden (life)?
2. Will you give up blaming, complaining, and explaining?
3. How will you sow more regularly? Lavishly? Fervently?
4. What will you sow today to reach your goal?

Soil questions focus attention.
1. What hard truths are you refusing to see or hear?
2. What limiting belief is wilting your commitment?
3. What weed-like distraction is choking your dream?
4. Are you settling or stretching?

Sickle questions strengthen determination.
1. What will your dream cost you?
2. What challenges do you foresee?
3. Are you prepared to pay the price and persevere?
4. Are the seeds you sow consistent with your desire?

God's Word says conditions are favorable for harvesting your dreams.

The GREENHOUSE *of the Soul*

"The most noteworthy thing about gardeners is that they are always optimistic, always enterprising, and never satisfied. They always look forward to doing something better than they have ever done before."
– Vita Sackville-West, English author and poet

Your life is constructed of choices that produce your character and circumstances. The goal of this book was to help you make the best possible choices. Mastering the moment of decision is the key to effective living. By linking cause and effect, you can dramatically and rapidly increase your success and satisfaction in life.

Choice involves weighing options and making a selection based on perceived benefits:

- A *bad* choice makes you less happy and productive.

- A *good* choice honors your principles and propels you toward your goal.

- A *great* choice pleases God, helps your fellow man and enlarges your soul.

But every life experience cannot be explained in terms of personal choice. Other factors are at work shaping your circumstances. In a fallen world where free wills collide, much that happens is not of your own choosing. For example, a farmer may sow good seed in the best possible soil, but the harvest will still depend on factors beyond his control. Storms, plagues and wars may deprive a hardworking farmer of the fruits of his labor. However, natural catastrophes and national conflicts do not have to destroy the farmer's faith (2 Corinthians 4:8-9; Romans 8:28).

In human affairs, crimes, quarrels, diseases, accidents and disasters are all part of the mix of life. Those who are victims of man's inhumanity or natural calamity should not conclude that they brought these sufferings upon themselves. Nonetheless, they are accountable for how they respond to trials. Adversity is the greenhouse of the soul and, quite possibly, the greatest opportunity you have for glorifying God (James 1:2-4).

The important question is, "What will you do with your sufferings and setbacks?" Will you make light of them or learn from them? Will you turn away from God or trust Him more than ever? Will you grow bitter from your losses or more thankful for your blessings? Will the death of a loved one become the moment you quit living, or will you embrace those who remain with new appreciation? In each case, faith tips the scale in favor of the most hopeful and courageous decision.

Every life situation presents you with a set of choices. Drawing from the parable of the sower, this book unearthed eight principles to explain how you can maximize those choices. Those who ignore these laws do so to their own detriment. Rather than fulfilling their dreams, they frustrate them. They turn the Seed Principle on its head and live instead by the Weed Principle. Weeds are the negative results that grow when people fail to:

1. Decide what they want (The Law of Causation)

2. Accept responsibility (The Law of Creation)

3. Grow inwardly (The Law of Cultivation)

4. Finish what they start (The Law of Continuation)

5. Live thoughtfully (The Lesson of the Hard Ground)

6. Put forth sufficient effort (The Lesson of the Rocky Ground)

7. Focus on what matters (The Lesson of the Thorny Ground)

8. Pursue their dreams wholeheartedly (The Lesson of the Good Ground)

The Weed Principle explains why people do not succeed in life. The problem is that they make choices that oppose their interests. They think, speak and behave in ways that do not create their best possible lives. The Seed Principle reveals why other people enjoy fruitful lives. It is because they make choices that align with God's will, the needs of their fellow man, and their own highest good. So, how do you want to spend your life, and what kind of influence would you like to have on those around you?

Great choices lie beyond the pursuit of self-indulgence and personal pleasure. They arise from a combination of three things:

- An enlightened mind;

- An empathetic heart; and

- An elevated will.

When clarity, compassion and character are lacking, disappointment is sure to follow. But when the heart, mind and will work in harmony, the result is increased happiness and productivity.

The gospel is God's means for restoring your spiritual integrity. It contains the power to set you free from thinking that limits your joy and usefulness. Through believing and obeying the gospel, sins are forgiven, hearts are healed, and choices are refined.

So, now that the secrets of the sower have been entrusted to you, what will you do with them? Will you let birds and rocks and thorns keep you from the harvest you desire? Or will you cultivate a good and noble heart and begin sowing the life of your dreams? Each day presents you with fresh opportunities for making exceptional choices that will produce a remarkable life. Do not waste your time or your mind. You have but one life, and what is your life but your choices?

"I call heaven and earth as witnesses today against you, that I have set before you life and death, blessing and cursing; therefore choose life, that both you and your descendants may live; that you may love the Lord your God, that you may obey His voice, and that you may cling to Him, for He is your life and the length of your days."
(Deuteronomy 30:19-20)

Answers to QUESTIONS

Chapter 1
1. The ability to make excellent choices
2. Because every decision has a real-life consequence
3. Regret and frustration
4. Joy and effectiveness
5. The Bible
6. It came from our Creator; it is inspired; it has a proven track record
7. Because no force on earth can generate good fruit like God's Word
8. Your heart
9. How you can live the most successful life possible
10. The parable of the sower

Chapter 2
1. Everything brings forth after its kind (Genesis 1:11-12)
2. They contain life
3. Likeness or identity (they replicate)
4. Biological and ideological
5. Water that runs down a dam's spillway
6. Water that turns a dam's turbines
7. A mustard seed
8. Faith
9. Foundational beliefs that form a person's worldview
10. Purpose, values, individuality, utility

Chapter 3
1. God has placed the future in my hands
2. Calamities of nature and collapses of social responsibility

3. Lost (disoriented)
4. Good planning (keeping the end in mind)
5. The outgrowth of aspiration and the fruit of faith
6. Making more and more good choices
7. Which is the longest and most difficult path?
8. Which path leads to my desired destination?
9. What you do with a choice after it is made
10. Clear objectives and obstinate effort

Chapter 4
1. Where native plants cease biological activity
2. To generate life (provide a creative environment for growth)
3. The mind, heart and will (cognition, emotion, volition)
4. Birds, rocks and thorns
5. Something is restricting or interfering with the growth of the seed
6. The receptivity and productivity of the human heart
7. Stolen, scorched, strangled
8. A committed marriage, a loving home, a caring church
9. The human heart
10. A shut mind, a shallow mind and a scattered mind

Chapter 5
1. Results
2. Incrementally and imperceptibly
3. A lot of patience and diligence
4. Downsize their dreams
5. The fruit of the Spirit
6. The product I desire; the process it requires; the promise God inspires
7. Thinking, speaking, writing, sharing
8. Firmly but flexibly
9. Help
10. Increase the number and power of reasons for reaching completion

Chapter 6
1. Four (wayside, rocky, thorny and good)
2. The hardened path between seed plots
3. Hardened hearts (lack of spiritual awareness or sensitivity)
4. The Word of God
5. It was trampled down, and birds devoured it
6. It was not tilled and prepared to receive the seed
7. The evil one
8. Wicked, Satan, devil
9. Immediately

10. Lest they should believe and be saved

Chapter 7
1. Soul conditioning
2. A sin-reduced, love-enriched heart
3. A ledge of rock was hidden beneath the surface
4. It withered
5. Because it lacked moisture
6. The rock blocked the roots from reaching water
7. When the sun reached its peak
8. Trials
9. A person who falls away in time of difficulty
10. Tribulation, persecution and temptation

Chapter 8
1. Thorns
2. They were choked
3. Cares, riches and pleasure
4. The cares of this world
5. They deceive
6. Maturing
7. Test or train
8. Good
9. In infirmities, reproaches, needs, persecutions and distresses for Christ's sake
10. Make a person better (stronger, holier, more Christlike)

Chapter 9
1. Good ground
2. A hundredfold
3. A good and noble heart
4. Keep it
5. They bear fruit
6. Patience
7. More thinking and better thinking
8. The optimal learning, working and growing mindset
9. The unleashing of potential through the unshackling of the heart
10. "He who has ears to hear, let him hear!"

Chapter 10
1. Angels and demons, deceased but living persons, God the Father, Son and Spirit
2. Paradise, heaven and hell
3. Souls, sin and love
4. By faith

5. Faith is the substance of things hoped for, the evidence of things not seen
6. Practice them
7. The choices you have made across the span of your lifetime
8. Your attitude
9. Prison
10. Reflection, responsibility, resolve, resilience

Chapter 11

1. The world
2. People
3. Sowing seeds of love
4. Sowing seeds of hatred
5. Consider sowing different seeds
6. Blame your spouse for depriving you of happiness
7. Make constructive changes in your own thinking and behavior
8. To value another by giving him or her your time and attention
9. You are not important to me
10. To contribute something of value to another's life

Chapter 12

1. Become a bigger person
2. He is too needy to attend to the needs of others
3. He can devote his attention to the concerns of his followers
4. By going before his followers
5. Character and competence
6. They distract them and deplete their spiritual energy
7. Teaching by example
8. A shortage of commitment
9. Gratitude
10. Sowing continuously, bountifully and fervently

Chapter 13

1. A hard path, a hidden rock and a useless thorn
2. Faith, follow-through and focus
3. Hope fulfillment
4. God will come to your aid
5. Faith
6. Blind or make-believe faith
7. Legitimate faith
8. Your values
9. Because they require added faith to endure and overcome
10. To make better choices